TABLE OF CONTENTS

Preface ... iv
Introduction: A Land of Many Names ... v

Chapter One: The Original Islanders ... 1
Chapter Two: Jacques Cartier Explores the Island ... 9
Chapter Three: First Settlements ... 15
Chapter Four: The Deportation ... 27
Chapter Five: A British Colony ... 37
Chapter Six: Pioneer Life ... 57
Chapter Seven: Island Politics and the Land Problem ... 79
Chapter Eight: Confederation ... 95
Chapter Nine: Prosperity and Decline ... 109
Chapter Ten: Island Life at the Turn of the Twentieth Century ... 125
Chapter Eleven: The Empire at War ... 147
Chapter Twelve: The Interwar Years: Good Times, Hard Times ... 159
Chapter Thirteen: The Second World War ... 179
Chapter Fourteen: Contemporary Political and Economic Issues ... 187
Chapter Fifteen: Contemporary Island Life ... 205

Appendix: A History of Prince Edward Island in Postage Stamps ... 214
Image Sources ... 218

PREFACE

The following account is my interpretation of Prince Edward Island history; it includes what I consider to be the Island's most important and compelling stories. It is written for the general reader, the interested tourist, and the amateur historian. For more detailed information on Prince Edward Island I urge you to subscribe to *The Island Magazine*, which publishes interesting and informative articles on virtually every aspect of Island history, geography, and culture. For the area in which *The Island Magazine* is weakest, modern Prince Edward Island, Edward MacDonald's *If You're Stronghearted: Prince Edward Island in the Twentieth Century* provides a well-researched, enjoyable read. The *Dictionary of Canadian Biography*, which is available online, is another excellent source.

Many people helped shape this book. Georges Arsenault provided me with his expertise on Island Acadians. Tammy MacDonald of the Mi'kmaq Confederacy on Prince Edward Island edited an early draft of the sections on the Mi'kmaq and added her own insights. Mary Juanita Rossiter read the entire manuscript and provided useful suggestions. As usual, Ken Shelton was of invaluable assistance with the visuals and contemporary Island matters. Deirdre Kessler made a thorough read-through of the first draft and suggested additional sources.

INTRODUCTION
A Land of Many Names

When Anne Shirley first arrived on Prince Edward Island in Lucy Maud Montgomery's novel *Anne of Green Gables*, she exclaimed, "I just love it already, and I'm so glad I'm going to live here. I've always heard that Prince Edward Island was the prettiest place in the world, and I used to imagine I was living here, but I never really expected I would. It's delightful when your imaginations come true, isn't it?"

With its quilt-like patchwork of farms, brightly painted fishing boats, blue ocean, sand-dune formations, and reddish soil, it's no wonder that Montgomery described Prince Edward Island as "the prettiest place in the world." The Island is as picturesque as it is enchanting. Island flowers are alive with colours in the spring, when temperatures range from eight to twenty-two degrees Celsius. Summers are warm, but rarely humid. Daytime temperatures are usually in the twenties and the coastal waters are ideal for swimming. Autumns are mainly clear and bright, with warm afternoons and cool evenings. Winters are long, with frequent snowstorms and temperatures ranging from minus three to minus eleven degrees.

Islanders cherish their history, and each community seems to have a book devoted to its long history. Genealogy is a popular pastime. Local radio stations include short vignettes on Island history. Popular storytellers and historians like Georges Arsenault, David Weale, and Boyde Beck enthrall Islanders with their writings, talks, and performances. Historic buildings, pioneer villages, museums, monuments, and cairns dot the province. Even automobile license plates make reference to important events in the province's history.

Each of Prince Edward Island's unofficial "names" describes an aspect of the province's history. At one time or another, the province has been known as:

- Abegweit (Mi'kmaq for "Cradled on the Waves")
- Minegoo (Mi'kmaq for "The Island")
- Île Saint-Jean
- New Ireland
- St. John's Island
- Garden of the Gulf
- The Denmark of Canada
- The Million-Acre Farm
- The Land of Anne
- The Home of Anne of Green Gables
- The Cradle of Confederation
- The Birthplace of Confederation
- Spud Island
- The Kentucky of Canada
- The Tuna Capital of the World
- *The* Island (to Islanders living away)

Islanders are proud of their heritage. When Governor General Lord Dufferin visited Charlottetown shortly after the Island entered Confederation in 1873, he was so impressed by the Islanders' sense of independence that he felt as if it were "the Dominion that has been annexed to Prince Edward Island." Two decades later, Lucy Maud Montgomery described this sense of uniqueness another way: "He said he was from 'the island!' What island, queried a listener? 'What island?' repeated our honest countryman, in amazement, 'Why, Prince Edward Island, man! What other Island is there?'"

What follows is an overview of Prince Edward Island's unique past. It explores the fascinating history of the early Aboriginal Peoples, the Mi'kmaq; the subsequent Acadian settlement and deportation; British settlement attempts and the ensuing problems of absentee landlords; and the Island's entry into Confederation. Later chapters chronicle the social, economic, and political developments of the Island from Confederation to the present. This is a story of fishers, farmers, shipbuilders, artists, and entrepreneurs, covering topics as diverse as silver foxes, *Anne of Green Gables*, Prohibition, iceboats and bridges, and political debate and turmoil.

CHAPTER ONE
The Original Islanders

What we know about the prehistory of Prince Edward Island has been pieced together from Aboriginal legends and the work of geologists, archaeologists, botanists, and climatologists. Most scientists believe that Prince Edward Island was slowly fashioned over centuries, and only comparatively recently has it been inhabited by humans.

The glaciers of the last ice age began to leave the Maritimes about eighteen thousand to thirteen thousand years ago. As the ice melted, the sea level rose, and Prince Edward Island was divided into three separate islands. Once the weight of the glaciers melted away, the land slowly rebounded. Over the next few thousand years the water retreated so far that the Island was joined to the mainland by a bridge of land approximately where Confederation Bridge is today, and the Northumberland Strait disappeared. Gradually, the water began to rise again, and about five thousand years ago the Island was again separated from the mainland by the Northumberland Strait.

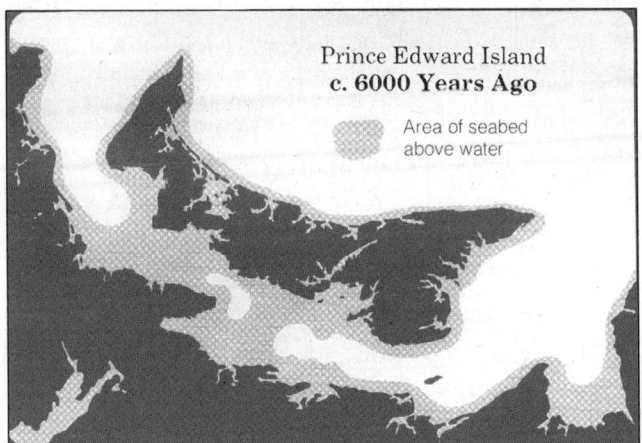

Prince Edward Island six thousand years ago, showing the parts of the seabed that were above water due to falling sea levels.

DINOSAURS ON THE ISLAND

A conceptual sketch of a Dimetrodon by Charles R. Knight

Discoveries in Nova Scotia in the past twenty years suggest that large mastodons inhabited the Maritimes between ten thousand and seventy thousand years ago. Perhaps the most fascinating discovery was the one made near New London, Prince Edward Island, in 1845. In the process of digging a well, several men uncovered the fossil of a *Bathygnathus borealis* that had been alive about 280 million years ago. This reptile, now called *Dimetrodon*, was about three metres long and had a large fin or "sail" on its back that was supported by bony spines. The sail kept the predator warm and limber in the cool early mornings while its prey was still sluggish.

Early Peoples

Human occupation of the Maritimes probably began about eleven thousand years ago, when Aboriginal Peoples migrated north from New England as the glaciers receded. The oldest known location of these peoples in Prince Edward Island is the Jones Site in Greenwich National Park, which has been carbon-dated at nine thousand to ten thousand years old. Since the early Aboriginals preferred to be near water, many of their campsites are now underwater, as soil erosion and the gradually rising sea levels have submerged the area's coastlines over time. The Jones Site, for example, which was excavated first in 1913 and again in the 1980s, is now below water.

When the early Aboriginals—whom archaeologists refer to as Paleo-Indians—came to the area now known as Prince Edward Island, it was joined to the mainland, the climate was much colder, and the vegetation was sparser than it is today. To survive, these Aboriginal Peoples hunted caribou, arctic foxes, and hares, and took advantage of the variety of fish and birds that frequented the area. Little is known about the Paleo-Indians, but artifacts found near Souris and East Point show that these hunters used triangular-bladed spear points and stone-tipped harpoons to kill their prey.

From nine thousand to thirty-five hundred years ago, during a period called the Maritime Archaic Age, Aboriginal Peoples with a more developed culture inhabited the Maritimes. They fashioned delicately carved bone, ivory, and stone figures of birds and whales, and made bone whistles and hair combs. Their way of life was more sea-oriented than that of earlier Aboriginal Peoples on the Island; they caught fish and sea mammals along the coast and fished along the rivers.

> **MI'KMAQ CREATION LEGEND**
> According to Mi'kmaq legend, the Great Spirit shaped a large piece of dark red clay into the form of a crescent with green grass, lush forests, and brightly coloured flowers to serve as a home for his Mi'kmaq people. The Great Spirit then placed it in the middle of the singing waters—the Gulf of St. Lawrence.

About twenty-five hundred years ago, temperatures increased significantly and a mixed forest of oak, elm, and maple emerged. The Aboriginal Peoples who occupied the land during this period practised an elaborate burial ritual in which they buried prized objects in large circular mounds about twelve metres in diameter. It is believed that these peoples were the ancestors of the First Nations peoples who now inhabit the Maritimes.

The Mi'kmaq

Approximately two thousand years ago, environmental conditions in the Maritimes were similar to today's. The region was populated by the Maliseet and Mi'kmaq peoples, who numbered between ten thousand and thirty-five thousand at this time. Archaeologists have discovered early Mi'kmaq sites in the areas around Malpeque, Rustico Bay, Savage Harbour, and in the North and South Lakes region.

The Mi'kmaq had a special relationship with nature. Humans were not considered superior to animals; they were equal partners with the animals as well as with the sun, the wind, and the rain. All animate and inanimate objects in the Mi'kmaq world had a spirit. They were so close to the animals they hunted that they could imitate their sounds. Hunters apologized to an animal for taking its life and treated the dead animal's carcass with respect, handling it according to prescribed rituals lest its spirit warn its fellows to leave the area. The bones of a bear, for example, were not to touch the ground, and the skulls of bears and beavers were carefully cleaned and placed

THE PEOPLE

The Mi'kmaq greeted Europeans by saying "Nikmaq," which means "my close relatives." French settlers referred to the Mi'kmaq as "notres nikmaqs," or "our brothers." Eventually, "nikmaq" was anglicized to "Micmac," which, until the 1980s, was their "official" name to English-speakers. Mi'kmaq is pronounced mig-maw, and is a plural form. The Mi'kmaq refer to themselves as "L'nu'k," which means "the people."

high on a pole or in a tree where dogs could not defile them. According to legend, the Great Spirit told the Mi'kmaq: "If you have to kill a deer for its meat and hide, you should tell the deer that its beauty will live on in the clothing that will be made out of its skin. The skin must be carefully treated and decorated so that it is worthy of the Great Spirit."

The Mi'kmaq were skilled craftspeople. They made wooden cradleboards that rested on mothers' backs, supported by a strap across their foreheads. This left their arms free for work and protected the children from tree branches. Inside the wigwam, the cradleboard was propped up so the infant could see its surroundings. With similar ingenuity, the Mi'kmaq crafted spears, bows and arrows, traps, axes, snowshoes, and toboggans. They turned bone points into harpoons, awls, and needles. The women scraped, tanned, and smoked animal hides to fashion clothes, which they decorated with beautiful geometric patterns and designs, and fashioned mats and containers out of reeds. Everyone in the village co-operated to build weirs (an enclosure of stakes in the river) to catch eels, salmon, shad, smelt, and other migrating fish.

Seasonal Lifestyle

Summers were the easiest time of year for the Mi'kmaq. They moved near the coast, where they lived in oblong wigwams that housed up to two dozen people. Food sources were abundant in the summer, and the Mi'kmaq gathered berries, mussels, clams, snails, oysters, and lobsters. Waterfowl were also plentiful. To catch ducks and geese at night, the Mi'kmaq disguised canoes to look like logs drifting on the tide. Once they had manoeuvred a canoe amidst the birds, the hunters lit torches and held them high above their heads. The startled birds flew in circles around the lights, and the hunters knocked them out of the air with clubs. The Mi'kmaq also hunted moose and deer during the summer months. Hunters stalking moose or deer disguised themselves in animal skins and used spears and arrows to shoot the animals.

Summer was the time when the Mi'kmaq gathered together in large groups to renew friendships, engage in storytelling, find mates, perform religious ceremonies, play games, and dance to bone flutes and rattles made of fish skins filled with small stones. One popular Mi'kmaq game involved tossing a ball stuffed with animal hair and grass between players. The object was to touch the ball against the opposing team's post at the end of the playing field.

The summer months were also used to form military alliances and raid other villages. Before warriors departed, the village held a feast and performed a war dance. The warriors carried wooden shields, clubs, knives, and bows and arrows.

Since autumn brought severe storms, the Mi'kmaq loaded their belongings into canoes and moved inland. Travelling in small groups of closely related families, they made their fall homes on the banks of fast-flowing streams, where they netted eels on their way to spawn. Hunters lured moose by imitating the cow's call and caught beavers by destroying their dams and clubbing them on dry land. The women smoked the meat from these animals to preserve it for the winter, and used the hides for making warm clothing or thongs to lace snowshoes and construct toboggans. They used the bones and tendons to sew together skins to make clothes and tools.

Winter posed the greatest challenge for the Mi'kmaq, who spent those months in the forests in small family groups, living in small, conical-shaped wigwams that sheltered approximately a dozen people. Inside, they lined the walls with animal hides to keep the wigwam warm and cozy and placed mats made of fir boughs or hides on the floor to make it more comfortable. Each family member had a special place in the wigwam: parents sat at the back, young children stayed next to their parents—girls on one side, boys on the other—and older children remained near the entrance. Individuals sat near the fire when they wanted to socialize.

During the winter, fishers cut holes in the ice to spear fish, and hunters on snowshoes ran down moose and deer in the deep snow. They also visited the coast to hunt seals. Beaver was another animal the Mi'kmaq could hunt during wintertime. After their dogs located a beaver lodge, the Mi'kmaq cut holes in the ice of the pond and then destroyed the lodge. When the beavers emerged from these holes, the hunters shot them with arrows tipped with harpoon heads. The Mi'kmaq women accompanied the hunters on the hunt and butchered the large animals on the spot before carrying the meat back to camp. When they arrived back at camp, the women roasted the meat on an open fire or boiled it in wooden bowls.

The Mi'kmaq eagerly awaited spring, when birds and waterfowl returned from the south and families made plans to return to their summer homes. Since birch bark peeled easily from the trees in the spring, the Mi'kmaq built their birchbark canoes at this time. These three- to nine-metre-long canoes were made of cedar. The Mi'kmaq stitched together bark sheets and fastened them to the wooden canoe frames using white spruce roots. Women and girls chewed spruce gum to make it pliable, then boiled it with fat and used it to waterproof the seams. The canoes' distinctive wide-bottomed, hump-backed design was not only light, but also sturdy enough to cross the Northumberland Strait to Cape Breton.

As the summer approached, Mi'kmaq women covered the wigwams with woven reeds or grass mats. When the weather was dry, the reeds shrank, allowing more air to flow through the mats, which kept the wigwam interior cool and free of smoke. When it rained, the reeds swelled and made the wigwam watertight. To make the wigwam more comfortable, the Mi'kmaq women covered the floor with spruce or fir boughs, leaving a space in the middle for an open fire.

Springtime food supplies consisted of fish, muskrats, and waterfowl. Hunters lured ducks onto small lakes using decoys and shot them with bows and arrows. As spring drew to a close, the bands moved to good fishing locations near the coast where there was sufficient space for everyone to gather for the summer.

Micmac Indians near Halifax *by John George Toler, 1808. The animal in the foreground is a distinctive breed of Mi'kmaq dog, which is known for its sharp-pointed ears and curling tail.*

Mi'kmaq Government

The nature of Mi'kmaq society included sharing and co-operation. They treated everyone as equals. Seldom did one person tell another what to do. Mi'kmaq society relied upon voluntary co-operation for the achievement of group goals. Individuals were free to do as they wished, although custom and tradition acted as strong deterrents.

Each clan or band was independent and was led by a chief whose job was to ensure the welfare of his people. This position was inherited from father to son, but could also be passed to another worthy male relative if no suitable son was available. Chiefs could also take more than one wife to ensure that the band would have a suitable leader. Each clan had its own symbol, which members of the clan used to mark wigwams, canoes, and clothing.

In the summer, when nearby tribes gathered together to renew friendships, a council of elders governed the gathering. In the spring or fall, band chiefs gathered to discuss important matters. The chief who presided over the district council was the eldest male of the most influential Mi'kmaq family in the district. Only men and boys who had killed their first moose could speak in the district councils, which assigned hunting and fishing territories and decided on matters that were important to the group. The Mi'kmaq were a loose confederacy that was divided into seven districts throughout the Maritimes and bound together through a common system of patrilineal clans. Periodically, the district chiefs met in a grand council to resolve issues that could cause serious conflict among the districts or with other Aboriginal Peoples. All discussions were based on consensus. If necessary, the grand council also elected one of its members to act as its spokesperson with outsiders.

Chapter Two
Jacques Cartier Explores the Island

Italian mariner Cristoforo Colombo (Christopher Columbus) believed that it was possible to sail west across the Atlantic Ocean to Asia. After Portugal rejected his plan to search for a northwest passage to Asia, Columbus won the support of King Ferdinand and Queen Isabella of Spain. In 1492, with a letter of introduction from the Spanish monarchy to "the Great Khan of China," Columbus set sail. Columbus wandered far off course, and after seventy days, rather than the week he expected, he landed on the island shared today by Haiti and the Dominican Republic. Thinking that he had found India, Columbus called the inhabitants "Indians."

Over the next few decades, other Spanish explorers followed Columbus to this "New World." The vast amounts of gold and silver that the Spanish explorers discovered there made Spain the envy of other nations, and England, Portugal, and France soon hired their own explorers to find kingdoms as rich as those that the Spaniards were exploiting in Central and South America. In 1534, King François I of France instructed explorer Jacques Cartier "to discover certain islands and land where it is said that a great quantity of gold, and other precious things are to be found" and to seek a route to Asia. Cartier subsequently became the first European to leave a written record of Prince Edward Island.

Cartier's Voyage
Cartier and his sixty-one men, some of whom were criminals released from jail for this voyage, set sail from St. Malo, France, in two vessels on April 20, 1534. Following a remarkably quick trip of only twenty days, they arrived in Newfoundland. After exploring the west coast of Newfoundland, Cartier sailed to the Magdalen Islands in the Gulf

of St. Lawrence, where he encountered "many great beasts, like large oxen, which have two tusks in their jaws like elephants' tusks, and swim about in the water." These were sea cows or walruses.

EARLY EXPLORERS OF NORTH AMERICA
- 1000: Norse (Vikings) visit Newfoundland
- 1492: Christopher Columbus lands in America
- 1497: John Cabot arrives in Newfoundland
- 1500: Gaspar Corte-Real visits Cape Breton
- 1513: Vasco Núñez de Balboa sights the Pacific Ocean from Panama
- 1520: Joao Alvares Fagundes visits Cape Breton
- 1521: Hernando Cortes conquers the Aztec empire
- 1524: Giovanni da Verrazzano explores the east coast of North America
- 1532-33: Francisco Pizarro conquers the Incas
- 1534: Jacques Cartier lands on Prince Edward Island
- 1536: Cartier makes a second voyage to Eastern Canada
- 1541-42: Cartier undertakes an expedition with Sieur Roberval
- 1577: Martin Frobisher visits Frobisher Bay
- 1604: Samuel de Champlain visits Nova Scotia
- 1610: Henry Hudson explores Hudson Bay
- 1610: John Guy establishes a colony in Newfoundland

Cartier sighted Prince Edward Island on June 29, 1534. He spent the next two days exploring the north coast, "the best-tempered region one can possibly see," which he believed was part of the mainland. Cartier wrote a vivid description of the landscape:

> We landed that day in four places to see the trees which were wonderfully beautiful and very fragrant. We discovered that there were cedars, yew-trees, pines, white elms, ash trees, willows and others, many of them unknown to us and all trees without fruit. The soil where there are no trees is also very rich and is

covered with pease, white and red gooseberry bushes, strawberries, raspberries and wild oats like rye.... It is the best tempered region one can possibly see and the heat is considerable.

Cartier's account was first published in Italian (in 1565), and later in English (1580), and in French (1598). However, the originals have disappeared over the years, and historians are unsure if Cartier actually wrote the manuscript.

After exploring several inlets along the coast of the Island in search of a passage to Asia, only to be "grieved and displeased," Cartier sailed to the Gaspé Peninsula on July 14, 1534, where he made contact with the Iroquois, erected a nine-metre-high cross, and claimed the land for King François I. He returned to France on July 25, along with two Aboriginals whom he hoped would serve as future interpreters. At that time it was common practice for explorers to kidnap Aboriginal Peoples, many of whom were later paraded about like zoo specimens. Most of these captives died from tuberculosis soon after being abducted.

Cartier made two subsequent trips to the New World in 1536 and 1541, but except for European fishing boats that may have stopped to trade with the Mi'kmaq or to collect drinking water and make repairs, Europeans did not revisit Prince Edward Island for another sixty years.

A portrait of Jacques Cartier by Théophile Hamel, circa 1844. This portrait was copied from an 1839 painting by Francois Riss, who apparently based his portrait on an old sketch in the Bibliothèque nationale de France. There are no authenticated portraits of Jacques Cartier.

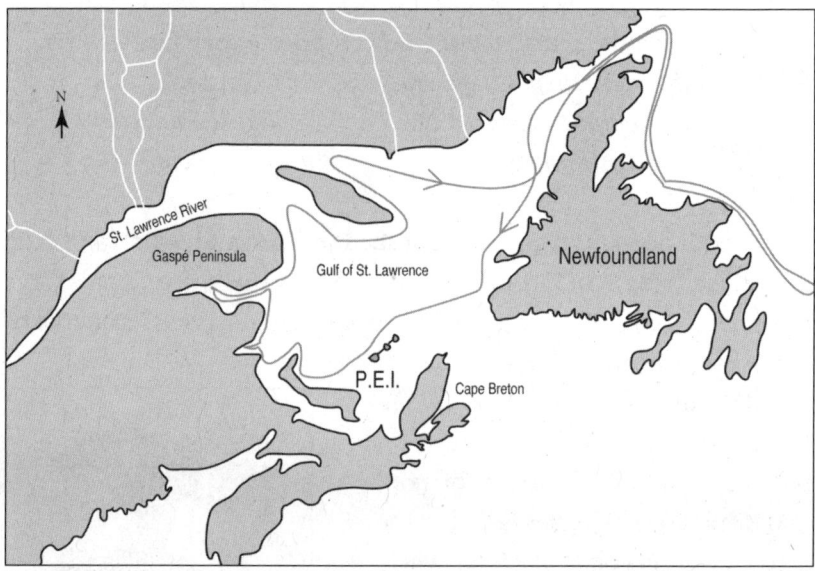

Cartier's route during his exploration of the New World in 1534.

New World, New Resources

Although the European explorers did not find silks, spices, or precious metals in North America, present-day Canada soon became very important to Europe. Fishing vessels from England, France, Spain, Portugal, and Holland came each year between March and October to catch cod in the Grand Banks, the Gulf of St. Lawrence, and the Bay of Fundy. Soon, approximately ten thousand fishers were sailing to the Grand Banks each year. The cod were so numerous that they sometimes slowed the progress of the fishers' ships.

When a good fishing location was discovered, the fleet captain established a temporary camp on the nearest shore. Here, the fish were dried on wooden drying racks, salted, and packed in barrels for the long journey back to Europe. While the fishers were on shore, they often traded with the Mi'kmaq, who exchanged beaver, caribou, otter, and other furs for guns, metal tools, axes, kettles, and bright clothing. These furs were used to make hats, muffs, gloves, coats, and fur-trimmed clothes, which commanded high prices in Europe for their warmth, beauty, and durability.

NO THOUGHT OF CONSERVATION

When Samuel de Champlain sailed to North America in 1603, he described how sailors dangled baited fishhooks in the air and seized birds by the legs when they swooped down to eat the bait. He complained that the noise of the whales and porpoises in the Gulf of St. Lawrence disturbed his sleep.

Earlier, Cartier had noted that some birds off the coast of Newfoundland were "as large as geese, being black and white with a beak like a crow," and wrote, "They are always in the water, being unable to fly, since they have tiny wings about half the size of your hand.... These birds are marvelously fat...and in less than half an hour our longboats were loaded with them. Each of our ships salted four or five casks, not to mention those we ate fresh." Easy to catch, tasty to eat, and good for fishing bait, the last of these great auks was killed in 1844. Cartier also noted the "infinite number of wood pigeons" in the area. These passenger pigeons were so numerous that migrating flocks eclipsed the sun for hours and the noise of their wings sounded like thunder. However, as a result of overhunting and a loss of habitat, the Island's passenger pigeon population soon died out. The last passenger pigeon reported on the Island was about 1890. Twenty-four years later, the last of its kind, a twenty-nine-year-old female passenger pigeon named Martha, died in a Cincinnati zoo.

The walrus fared only slightly better. Thousands of walruses lived in the shallow coastal waters on Prince Edward Island's north shore in the seventeenth century. They were prized for their oil, their ivory tusks (termed "white gold"), and their hides. They were hunted remorselessly, and although the Island government attempted to regulate the sea cow fishery in 1770, walruses barely survived another decade. In 1839, the species was officially declared extinct in the region. By this time, humans had also hunted the Island's caribou and wolf populations to extinction.

Fish was a major part of most Europeans' diets. In addition to Fridays, there were about 150 days each year when Roman Catholics were not supposed to eat meat. Fish was thus a major contributor to Europe's economy. France, for example, made more money importing fish from the New World than it did selling beaver furs. Because fish was also important to Great Britain's economy, the British government created fish days to encourage its consumption. The importance of fish to these countries' economies helps explain why England and

France fought for control of the Maritimes so frequently in the seventeenth and eighteenth centuries. Instead of coming to North America in search of a route to Asia, Europeans now came for fish and furs. Soon settlers would join the fishers and the fur traders.

CHAPTER THREE
First Settlements

In the sixty years following Jacques Cartier's visits to North America, only fishers and fur traders remained interested in the area. It wasn't until French explorer Samuel de Champlain's voyage to the New World in 1603 that European interest in the region was re-ignited.

During his initial explorations of the area, Champlain sailed up the St. Lawrence River to the present site of Montreal, where rapids prevented him from travelling farther west. Champlain returned to France convinced that he had found a route to China and subsequently told King Henry IV about his discoveries and the plentiful supply of valuable beaver furs in the area. Since permanent settlement was considered important in the international world as proof of ownership, King Henry had already decided to start a colony in North America and had granted Frenchman Pierre du Gua de Monts, whose bravery in fighting in French wars had attracted the court's attention, all of present-day Nova Scotia, New Brunswick, Prince Edward Island, and parts of Quebec and the eastern United States in return for settling the area. This ten-year grant included the exclusive right to fish and trade with the Aboriginals in return for de Monts's promise to bring at least sixty settlers to the area each year, explore the land, and introduce the Aboriginal inhabitants to Christianity.

SETTLEMENT TIMELINE

1605:	France founds Port-Royal
1713:	The Treaty of Utrecht is signed
1719–20:	The first settlers arrive on Île Saint-Jean
1720:	The construction of Louisbourg begins
1732:	Jean Pierre Roma arrives on Île Saint-Jean
1745:	Louisbourg is captured
1748:	The treaty of Aix-la-Chapelle returns Louisbourg to France
1749:	Halifax is founded
1754:	The Seven Years' War begins in North America
1755:	The Deportation of Acadians begins
1758:	Britain captures Louisbourg
1763:	The treaty of Paris cedes Île Saint-Jean to Britain

An engraving of Samuel de Champlain by Théophile Hamel, circa 1866

De Monts hired Champlain as his cartographer and in 1604 they sailed into the Bay of Fundy with about eighty settlers and their supplies. They decided to winter on Dochet's Island at the mouth of the St. Croix River on the present border between Maine and New Brunswick, as from there they could control access to the interior and its valuable resources. In addition, the thick, tall grass seemed to indicate fertile soil. However, the island turned out to be a poor choice. It had no fresh water and very little wood. The men had to cross to the mainland to hunt for food. The winter weather that year was very severe and icy winds whipped across the river and swept around the settlers' log cabins. Partway through the winter the firewood ran out. For the last half of the winter the colonists lived on salted meat and melted snow. Almost one-half of the men died as a result of the conditions.

In the spring, the remaining settlers moved across the Bay of Fundy to the mainland. De Monts recruited more people from France and established the colony of Port-Royal (now Annapolis Royal) in present-day Nova Scotia. With the help of the Mi'kmaq, who provided the settlers with food and assistance, Port-Royal survived. This was the first European agricultural settlement in Canada.

Settlement spread gradually, and by 1700 there were close to fifteen hundred people in the Maritimes. Fifty years later, the population reached eleven thousand. Good climate and diet, few epidemics, early marriages, and a low mortality rate combined to produce large families. Gradually, the settlers developed their own distinctive way of life and identity. They called their new home Acadie, and before long the people living in present-day Nova Scotia, New Brunswick, and Prince Edward Island were called Acadians.

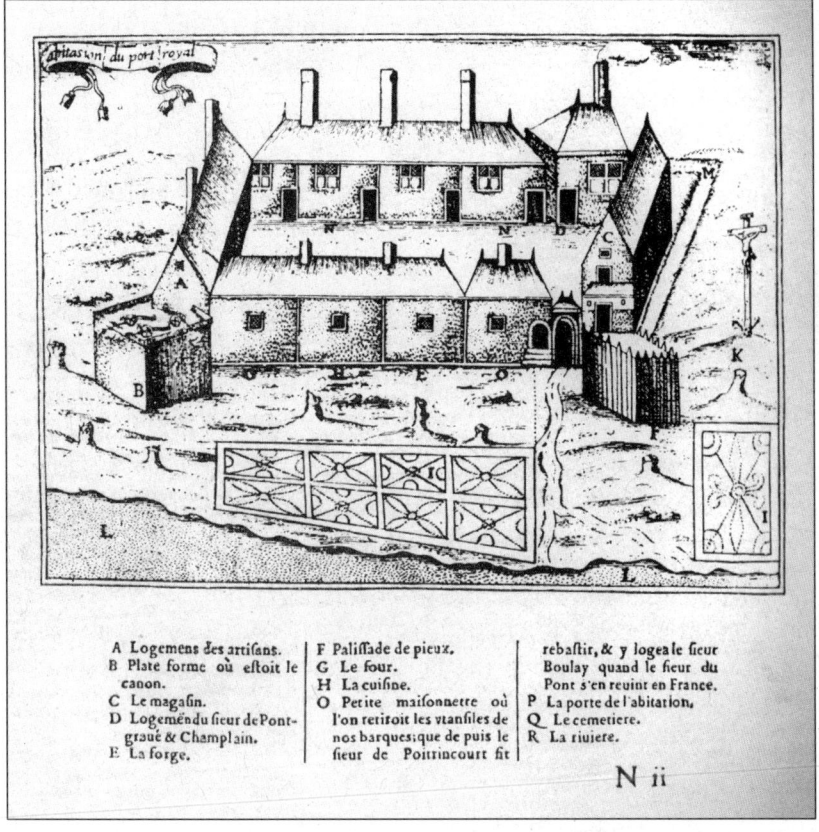

A sketch of the Port-Royal habitation drawn by Champlain in 1613. This drawing was used in the reconstruction of the Port-Royal National Historic Site in 1939.

ORIGINS OF THE NAME "ACADIA"

The origin of the word "Acadia" (or "Acadie") is a mystery. When Giovanni Verrazzano explored the east coast of North America in 1524, he used the name Arcadia in his diary in reference to the location in ancient Greece known for its contentment and innocence. Later, according to one theory, the "r" was dropped and gradually the word evolved from "Arcadia" to "La Cadie" to "L'Acadie." Another theory states that "Acadie" is derived from the Mi'kmaq word "quoddy" (or "cadie"), which means "fertile areas," as used in the names of such Nova Scotian locations as Shubenacadie, Tracadie, and Passamaquoddy.

A medal commemorating the Treaty of Utrecht, 1713

The Treaty of Utrecht

For most of the 1600s, England and France were at war in Europe, and these conflicts frequently spread to North America. France argued that because Jacques Cartier was the first European to land in Acadia, the area was French territory. England claimed that since John Cabot was the first European to discover Acadia, it belonged to England. Neither country was especially interested in establishing a colony in Atlantic Canada.

Although Acadia had good agricultural land, the region was considered more important for its position near the best fishing grounds in North America and for its strategic location at the entrance of the St. Lawrence River.

The year 1713 was a turning point in the history of Acadia. The Treaty of Utrecht, which ended the War of the Spanish Succession in 1713, changed the balance of power in North America. France kept New France (Quebec), Île Royale (Cape Breton), and Île Saint-Jean (Prince Edward Island), and secured the right to land and dry fish on the shores of Newfoundland between Cape Bonavista and Point Riche. England gained present-day Nova Scotia and the land claimed by the Hudson Bay Company, and kept Newfoundland. New Brunswick remained disputed land.

One problem that arose with the British acquisition of Nova Scotia was what to do with the French subjects who had settled there. According to the treaty, the Acadians living in Nova Scotia could "remove themselves within a year to any other place, as they shall think fit, together with their moveable objects." Those who chose to remain in Nova Scotia were granted freedom of religion, became subject to British laws, and were expected to swear allegiance to the British crown.

After the treaty was signed, France attempted to persuade the Acadians to move to Île Royale (Cape Breton) to strengthen that area against future British attacks. Britain did not want this to happen and thus allowed the Acadians to remain in Nova Scotia without adhering to the treaty and swearing their oaths of allegiance to the British crown. Most Acadians decided not to leave their homes in Nova Scotia for Île Royale, which suffered from frequent fogs and infertile soil, as they had put too much work into the land to leave. Britain had captured Acadia several times before and had returned it to France, and the Acadians thought that perhaps this was another one of these times.

Following the signing of the treaty, France began to make plans to build an impressive fortified town on Île Royale to protect New France and the fisheries from British attacks. Construction began in 1720 and continued for twenty-five years. According to folklore, King Louis XV of France joked that with all the money he had spent on its construction, he expected to see the fortress appear on the horizon. Louisbourg, as the town was named, was built on an ice-free harbour on the east coast of Île Royale that could shelter over a hundred ships. Louisbourg was at the centre of the lucrative cod fishery and had regular commercial contact with France, the West Indies, Quebec, and New England. By 1737, it was home to approximately 1,460 civilians and had a garrison of 540 soldiers.

First Settlements on Île Saint-Jean

Following Jacques Cartier's initial landing on Île Saint-Jean in 1534, Europeans largely ignored the Island. Fishers often landed on the Island to obtain fresh water, repair their ships, and dry their fish, but no one settled there. In 1604, King Louis XIV granted Île Saint-Jean to Pierre du Gua de Monts, but de Monts failed to bring the promised settlers to the Island. In 1653, France granted control of the Island to Nicolas Denys, a French explorer and entrepreneur, in return for his promise to establish a settlement. Ten years later, after Denys had failed to bring colonists to the

ORIGINS OF THE NAME "ÎLE SAINT-JEAN"

No one knows who first named Île Saint-Jean. Jacques Cartier thought the island was part of the mainland, so he obviously did not name it. The first written mention of Île Saint-Jean appeared on a 1601 map. The Island was probably named after Saint John the Baptist, since explorers and fishers often stopped there around the time of the saint's holiday on June 24.

Island, the king awarded it to Francois Doublet, a shipowner and merchant, with instructions to settle it. When Doublet also failed to live up to his promises, King Louis XV gave Île Saint-Jean to Gabriel Gauthier—with the same result.

By 1719 it was evident that few Acadians could be persuaded to leave their homes on the mainland for the poor agricultural land on Île Royale, and Louis XV decided to open Île Saint-Jean to Acadian settlement. He thought that if the Acadians would not leave their farms for Île Royale, perhaps they would come to Île Saint-Jean and provide needed food for the garrison at Louisbourg. The king granted the rights to Île Saint-Jean to Comte de Saint-Pierre, a well-connected courtier who had benefited from the successes of recent speculative schemes that exploited the natural resources of France's colonies. Saint-Pierre formed the Compagnie de l'Île Saint-Jean in 1719. In exchange for fishing rights to Île Saint-Jean and "adjacent islands," as well as the power to distribute land and collect rents, Saint-Pierre promised to settle one hundred people the first year and fifty each year thereafter until the Island was settled. In April 1720, Saint-Pierre sent approximately 250 French colonists to the Island with supplies of grain, livestock, tools, and clothing. Four months later, the ships arrived at Port-la-Joye (across the Hillsborough Harbour from present-day Charlottetown). Later, most of the colonists moved to Havre-Saint-Pierre (St. Peter's) where fishing was more lucrative.

Despite severe hardships, which included a mortality rate of approximately twenty percent from scurvy the first winter, the colonists built several vessels and sent one to France the next summer with a hold full of cod. In 1722, the colonists supplied dried cod and fish oil to Louisbourg and sent another shipment of cod to France. That same year, conflict with Île Royale fishers over fishing rights in the Gulf of St. Lawrence caused the Compagnie de l'Île Saint-Jean to arm two vessels and seize several Île Royale fishing boats. "Fish may be caught in abundance from a shallop, but if these individuals from Île Royale keep sending their schooners here to fish, as they did this year, the fishery will soon be ruined," wrote one Île Saint-Jean resident. Although France confirmed the company's control of the waters, few people came to Île Saint-Jean, and the settlement continued to cost more than it earned. When the Compagnie de l'Île Saint-Jean declared bankruptcy in 1724, its possessions were sold at an auction in Louisbourg and responsibility for Île Saint-Jean reverted to the authorities in Île Royale.

For the first time, there was a French presence on the Island, consisting of settlers from France and Acadians who had emigrated on their own initiative. The largest settlements on the Island were at Havre-Saint-Pierre, Tracadie, Savage Harbour, and Malpeque. Port-la-Joye, which France supplied with a small garrison of twenty-five men in 1726, was the capital of the Island. The population of the Island grew slowly, reaching 347 in 1732. Havre-Saint-Pierre was the Island's fishing capital. Since cod formed the basis of the Island economy, Havre-Saint-Pierre was also the commercial capital of the Island. The 1728 census noted that there were twenty-three homes in the Havre-Saint-Pierre area with 116 permanent settlers, most of whom were born in France. In the summers, fishers who came from France almost doubled the settlement's population.

Île Saint-Jean Census, 1734

Settlement	Families	Women	Boys +11	Boys -11	Girls	Servants	Fishermen	Total	Cattle	Sheep
Port-la-Joye	12	10	4	23	22	5	7	83	87	3
Rivière du Port-la-Joye	9	7	3	11	10	0	0	89	30	2
Havre-Saint Pierre	39	32	13	36	44	12	163	339	89	67
Havre à l'Anguille	4	4	1	12	5	0	0	26	13	8
Tracadie	5	5	1	11	13	1	0	86	54	18
Malpeque	4	4	3	6	5	0	0	22	56	21
Pointe de l'Est	3	2	0	1	1	0	6	13	0	0
Trois Rivières	1	0	1	0	1	11	0	14	3	0
Total	77	64	26	100	101	29	176	572	332	119

THE SEARCH FOR SUITABLE TREES

Because pine trees possessed the requisite suppleness, strength, durability, resin, and absence of knots, European shipbuilders used them to fashion masts for naval man-of-war vessels. It was of vital strategic importance to have a ready supply of suitable trees for this purpose, and pine thus became an important commodity during the eighteenth century. However, Europe's pine supplies were dwindling at this time and the wood was becoming more expensive, and the Europeans began looking for new sources of the commodity. North America's virgin stands of white and red pine offered what seemed to be an almost limitless supply.

In 1727, France ordered a survey of the pine trees in the Savage Harbour region of Île Saint-Jean. Jacques d'Espiet de Pensens led the survey expedition. Pensens, who had recently been made commandant at Île Saint-Jean, ordered the garrison soldiers to cut down a representative sample of pine trees, and later reported that they were "healthy, well grown and resinous, of a fine and tight grain, very supple, although some full of knots at 30 or 35 feet from the large end, generally straight...." When the first shipment reached France in 1728, however, the trees were discovered to be dry and full of knots, thus ending France's search for pine trees on the Island. In 1736 and 1742, large forest fires swept through the Island's best timber stands, ending the possibility of a prosperous timber trade.

Jean Pierre Roma's Island

In 1731, King Louis XV granted the Company of the East exclusive rights to the land drained by the Cardigan, Brudenell, and Montague rivers. In return for this 220-kilometre strip of coastline on the eastern part of the Island and permission to establish fish-drying facilities on the north shore at Havre-Saint-Pierre, the Company of the East agreed to bring out eighty settlers in 1732 and thirty more each subsequent year. Jean Pierre Roma, who was appointed a director of the company, was the moving spirit behind the venture and one of the few people who thought that Île Saint-Jean had a bright future.

Roma sailed into Cardigan Bay in June 1732 with three ships carrying livestock, tools, supplies, fishers, and *engagés*, who had signed up to work for eighteen to thirty-six months. He chose the land at present-day Trois Rivières to establish his colony.

Roma personally oversaw the settlement's growth. By August 1734, the men had improved the harbour by levelling the shoreline and building two piers, and had established a bakery, a forge, a stable, a large storehouse, and an ice house. The settlers cleared the nearby fields of timber and removed more than six thousand stumps—many of which were so heavy that a dozen men were required to move them. They also planted cabbages, turnips, wheat, and peas, and harvested the sea.

Since travel by water to other settlements on the Island was time-consuming and dangerous, the colonists blazed two-metre-wide bush paths through the wilderness to connect Trois Rivières with Cardigan, Souris, Sturgeon River, Havre-Saint-Pierre, and the garrison at Port-la-Joye. Roma sought to distract his men from the hard work and their low wages by arranging frequent feasts with singing and dancing.

LET THEM EAT BREAD

Bread was the single most important food in the settlers' diet. On average, one person consumed over a pound of bread each day. A typical loaf of bread weighed about six pounds and was eighty percent whole wheat and twenty percent rye. The Acadians' dietary staples consisted of pea soup; bread or porridge; salted or fresh beef, fish, pork, mutton, and fowl; and garden vegetables. Potatoes were not yet grown on the Island. The men smoked tobacco, and everyone chewed spruce gum to aid digestion and cleanse the teeth.

EARLY ISLAND SLAVERY

Although France sanctioned slavery in its colonies, slave holding in Acadia was expensive and slaves were valued more as a sign of status than for their economic benefits. In 1685, France decreed that slaves had to be baptized as Catholics; could only marry with their master's consent; could not carry a weapon; and should receive the death penalty for striking their masters. In addition, the children of slaves became the master's property. Although masters could whip their slaves, they could not imprison or execute them without the court's permission. On a more positive note, the law also required slave-owners to feed, clothe, and house their slaves, to care for them when they became old and sick, and not to separate young children from their parents.

It is not known how many black slaves lived in Île Saint-Jean. There were a few blacks in Roma's colony, and there are references to black slaves in Saint-Pierre-du-Nord and elsewhere.

Roma's Plan

Jean Pierre Roma wanted to make his settlement the centre of trade for the region. His plan was to transport fish to France in exchange for manufactured goods; send fish and lumber to the West Indies in return for sugar, molasses, and coffee; ship food to Louisbourg; and transport West Indies' sugar, molasses, and coffee to Quebec in exchange for biscuits and flour.

However, Roma was prone to conflict with his partners, government officials, and the clergy. Roma disliked the two priests who accompanied the first settlers to Trois Rivières. He described one as an Irish drunkard and the other as a Parisian troublemaker. Roma especially distrusted the Irish priest, Abbé de Bierne (Byrne), who insisted that the people should not be forced to work on Sundays and feast days. Roma stated that there was too much work to be done to allow for rest on Sundays, and argued that he had the king's authority to make laws for the colony. De Bierne claimed to have divine authority and informed the settlers that they were to follow his instructions in matters of religion. After a bitter struggle, Roma forced de Bierne to leave. Shortly afterwards, Roma dismissed the remaining priest and consolidated his control.

Bad luck plagued Roma's settlement. In 1736, fire destroyed most of the crops. Despite Roma's two years of hard work, the other directors of the Company of the East were not pleased with the colony's progress. Unwilling to weather a few more lean years, they refused to pay for additional provisions, and blamed Roma for the colony's lack of success. When the company decided to rid itself of this "burden," Roma assumed control of the colony in May 1737.

MOUSE INVASIONS

The Island settlers experienced several plagues of mice. When the snow was deep for several winters in a row, the mouse population multiplied rapidly. In the spring, starving mice marched out of the forest in long narrow columns and ate everything in their way. When they came to a river, the mice at the front of the lines were pushed on by those behind, and the river became choked with dead mouse bodies. So numerous were these tiny invaders that nearby ships were slowed by the masses of drowned mice. Plagues of mice destroyed Île Saint-Jean crops in 1724, 1728, 1738, and 1749. Each time this happened the settlers had to rely on Louisbourg for food and seeds. After the British assumed control of the Island, additional plagues occurred in 1770, 1775, 1782, and 1814.

THE ROMA RECONSTRUCTION

The Jean-Pierre Roma at Three Rivers National Historic Site

In 1933, Jean-Pierre Roma at Three Rivers National Historic Site, a reconstruction of the settlement that Jean-Pierre Roma established at Trois Rivières, became one of the earliest designated National Historic Sites of Canada. Today, few signs of Roma's efforts remain. Much of the original shoreline has washed away, and archaeological investigations at the site in 1968-70 revealed only a few foundation and masonry remnants. The recently renovated site offers a cluster of eighteenth-century-style buildings, costumed guides, picnic grounds, and historical reenactments.

The settlement's bad luck continued the next year when a plague of field mice ate the entire crop. Three years later, Roma's cargo vessel was shipwrecked. These disasters forced him to borrow money to keep the colony afloat. Finally, just when the future was beginning to look promising for Trois Rivières, British troops attacked and destroyed the French settlements at Port-la-Joye and Trois Rivières. The soldiers at Port-la-Joye managed to kill or wound nine British soldiers, but Roma's colony did not resist. Roma and his son and daughter watched helplessly from the forest as the British burned the settlers' homes and loaded the colony's livestock, tools, and grain aboard their ships. Roma walked to Havre Saint-Pierre, where he remained for a year before sailing to Quebec and, three years later, to the West Indies. Although the settlers slowly came back, Jean Pierre Roma never returned to Île Saint-Jean, despite his desire to do so. His work settling the Island would be continued by others.

Chapter Four
The Deportation

The British attacks at Port-la-Joye and Trois Rivières were part of the continuing struggle between France and Great Britain, which, at the time of the attacks, were rivals in the War of Austrian Succession. Britain and France distrusted each other. They both wanted to be powerful maritime nations with wealthy colonies scattered around the globe. Equally important, in a time when religion was paramount, one was Protestant and the other was Roman Catholic.

The War of the Austrian Succession began in Europe in 1744 and spread around the world. In North America, British colonists in New England wished to prevent the French and their Aboriginal allies from raiding and looting their villages. This meant capturing France's stronghold in the region—Louisbourg. In May 1745, soldiers from Britain and New England dragged cannons through the poorly protected marshland behind Louisbourg and besieged and captured the fortress.

However, the presence of the Roman Catholic Acadians—people who refused to swear allegiance to the British monarchy and bear arms on its behalf—in British territory was still a potential danger. Thus, after the British captured Louisbourg in July 1745, they deported approximately four thousand of its French soldiers and civilians back to France.

During the next three years, the British authorities made several attempts to deport the Île Saint-Jean Acadians, who numbered about one thousand. Fewer than three weeks after the fall of Louisbourg, Commodore Peter Warren ordered Captain Daniel Fones to sail to the Island and "There take on board and bring here all the French inhabitants and such of their effects as [he could] carry...," and to treat them "with the utmost civility and humanity." Unbeknownst to Warren, the captain who was to be in charge of the deportation had been killed in Cape Breton, and by the time Warren learned of this it was too late in the year to mount another campaign. Île Saint-Jean was spared—for the time being.

Although the residents of Île Saint-Jean promised to remain neutral, in August 1745, Governor William Shirley of Massachusetts, the architect of the siege of Louisbourg, ordered that the inhabitants of Île Saint-Jean and their effects be removed to Boston. This time, concern that French warships might be approaching Nova Scotia kept the proposed transport in harbour lest the ships be needed, and the Island Acadians were saved again.

However, Shirley was still determined to deport the Acadians from the Island, and in May 1746, he instructed them to prepare to be deported. This time, the Acadians were saved by a transfer of power from Shirley to Commodore Charles Knowles and Britain's decision to concentrate on capturing Quebec.

During the summer of 1746, French soldiers and their Mi'kmaq allies ambushed and killed about forty British soldiers at Port-la-Joye. In retaliation, the British authorities sent five hundred soldiers to punish the inhabitants. This time, the Acadians were saved by fog and strong winds, which prevented the British fleet from leaving Louisbourg for a week, by which time it was too late in the year for another attempt.

The Calm Before the Storm
The War of the Austrian Succession lasted four years. Neither side was completely victorious. Great Britain captured Louisbourg, but lost territory in other parts of the world. The Treaty of Aix-la-Chapelle in 1748 ended the war and returned Louisbourg to France in exchange for the Indian state of Madras. In North America, the situation reverted to what it had been in 1713; Île Saint-Jean remained under French control and Britain retained Nova Scotia.

The British colonies in New England were unhappy that Great Britain had returned Louisbourg to France, as it was from Louisbourg that the French directed many raids against New England. To satisfy the New England colonies, and to create a military presence in the

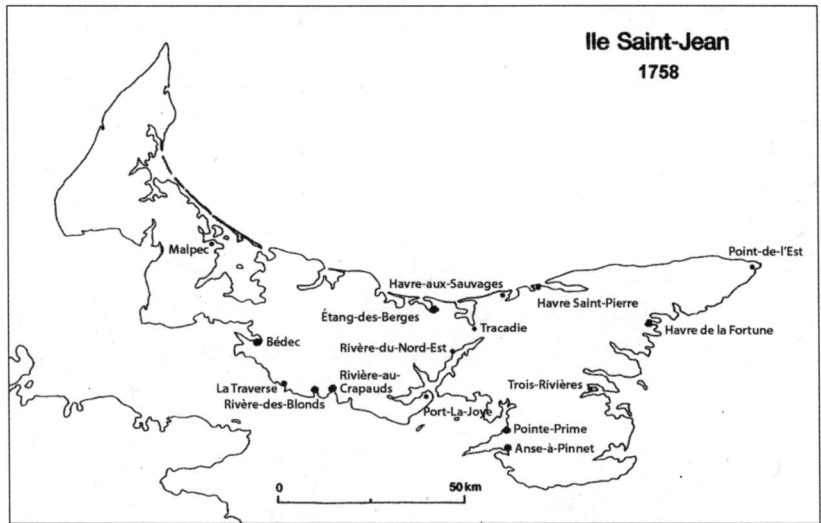

Major settlements on Île Saint-Jean, 1758

area, Great Britain established Halifax on the southeastern shore of Nova Scotia in 1749. Halifax was to be the beginning of a large-scale British settlement in Nova Scotia designed to eventually assimilate the Acadians.

After the Treaty of Aix-la-Chapelle, France began to take serious interest in Île Saint-Jean as a counterweight to the British presence in Nova Scotia. The mainland Acadians were still reluctant to move to the Island, but when Great Britain demanded that they promise to fight against their mother country in all future North American wars, many of them chose to move to Île Saint-Jean, settling in present-day Pownal, Orwell, Pinette, Crapaud, Tryon, Covehead, Johnstons River, and elsewhere on the Island. Although France still considered Île Saint-Jean second in importance to Louisbourg, it was finally showing signs of real growth, and the Island's population tripled to more than two thousand people in 1752.

So as not to distract Island settlers from growing food for Louisbourg, France allowed commercial fishing out of only two harbours on the Island. The Island, however, had few natural meadows, and to obtain adequate farmlands the Acadians were forced to clear forested areas, which was back-breaking work. Forest fires, wheat rust, and plagues of mice and grasshoppers were frequent occurrences and meant that only occasionally did Île Saint-Jean send livestock, grain, or vegetables to Louisbourg. Instead, Louisbourg often had to supply the settlers with food.

Le Grand Dérangement

The Seven Years' War pitted Great Britain and Prussia (now northern Germany) against France, Austria, Russia, and Sweden. Fighting took place in Europe, the Americas, and India, and on the Atlantic, Caribbean, Indian, and Mediterranean waters. The war in North America began in the Ohio region in 1754—two years before it commenced in Europe.

In the lead-up to the war, the rebuilding of Louisbourg and the construction of several forts on disputed land in Nova Scotia in 1750 signalled that France was still very much interested in Acadia. Equally worrisome to Britain was the Acadians' alliance with the Mi'kmaq, who harassed the colonists in Halifax and attacked the occasional British vessel. The Roman Catholic missionaries and priests in the area provided another British grievance, as in those days it was virtually impossible to separate religion from national loyalties. In addition, the bishops in New France (Quebec) were instructing the Catholic missionaries to encourage the Mi'kmaq to raid British settlements.

Charles Lawrence, the lieutenant-governor of Nova Scotia, viewed the priests as *agents provocateurs* and the Acadians as a potential fifth column in wartime. The latter worry seemed especially true when Britain discovered several hundred Acadians inside the French Fort Beauséjour, which lay on the border between New Brunswick and Nova Scotia, after its capture on June 16, 1755. The Acadians stated that France had forced them to help and that none of them had taken up arms against the British. They further argued that they had been neutral in the past and they would remain neutral in the future, but even before the fall of Fort Beauséjour, Lawrence had decided that the Acadians must choose a side.

According to international agreements and tradition, Britain had the right to insist on unconditional loyalty from its citizens. Thus, in early July 1754, Lawrence ordered the Acadians to send delegates to Halifax to meet with him. However, after news arrived that French troops had defeated a larger British regiment in the Ohio Valley, Lawrence informed the Acadian representatives who met with him that they must "resolve either to take the Oath without any Reserve or else quit their lands," because "Affairs were now at such a crisis in America that no delay could be admitted." Five times since 1713 the British governors of Acadia had attempted to persuade the Acadians to swear an unqualified oath of allegiance to the British monarch, and each time the Acadians had refused to agree to bear arms against either France or their Mi'kmaq allies. As a result, this time the Acadians probably underestimated Lawrence's determination to force them to sign the oath of allegiance.

Charles Lawrence, governor of Nova Scotia from 1756 to 1760

The Acadians thus refused to sign an unqualified oath of allegiance, which led Lawrence to make perhaps the most important decision in Maritime history. On July 28, 1755, he ordered his troops to round up all the Acadians in Nova Scotia, burn their homes, destroy their crops, and disperse them among England's colonies to the south. Although he did not consult with the officials in Great Britain about this decision, that fact that he was promoted governor of Nova Scotia the next year indicates that the British officials were not displeased by his actions.

Approximately seven thousand Acadians were deported in 1755, and thousands more were forced out of Nova Scotia over the following years. English-speaking historians usually refer to this event as the Deportation. Acadians call it *Le Grand Dérangement* (The Great Upheaval), which encompasses both the various deportations between 1755 and 1762 and the Acadians' subsequent search for a new homeland.

By the time the deportations ended in 1762, more than eleven thousand Acadians had been uprooted, many of whom had died of malnutrition and diseases caused by the unsanitary conditions aboard the British ships. Several thousand others escaped capture and made their way to French settlements in Île Saint-Jean, the Miramichi, and Quebec.

The arrival of some two thousand Acadian refugees on Île Saint-Jean brought total confusion. In the previous five years there had been only one good crop on the Island, and there was not enough food for everyone. Many of the newcomers arrived with only the clothes they were wearing. Families wandered from barn to barn, seeking food and shelter. Life was miserable, but it was preferable to being deported.

Deportations Continue on Île Saint-Jean

The British forces made their first major North American breakthrough in the Seven Years' War in June 1758, when thirty-nine ships and twenty-seven thousand men blockaded Louisbourg. After a seven-week siege, Louisbourg once again surrendered to the British. Shortly after Louisbourg surrendered, Major General Jeffrey Amherst, the commander of the British forces, ordered Lieutenant Colonel Andrew Rollo to capture the French garrison in Île Saint-Jean, return the Island Acadians to Louisbourg, and erect a fort. Rollo embarked for Île Saint-Jean in August 1758 with four transport ships, a schooner, the twenty-four-gun HMS *Hind*, five hundred soldiers, and enough materials to build a fort.

When Lord Rollo sailed into Hillsborough Bay on August 17, 1758, Port-la-Joye surrendered without firing a shot. Rollo allowed two priests from the Island to travel to Louisbourg to plead the Acadians' cause, but their pleas were ignored. The first of Rollo's transport ships returned to Louisbourg on September 4 with almost seven hundred Acadian passengers. The Acadians were subsequently sent to France, and the French military personnel were transported to England as prisoners of war. The British eventually rounded up and shipped about three thousand Acadians to France. Similar to the Nova Scotia Acadians, the inhabitants of Île Saint-Jean were allowed to pack only their clothes, bedding, and a few personal belongings; livestock, tools, dishes, and the rest of their possessions were left behind for the conquerors. Unlike the situation on the mainland, the British soldiers did not deliberately destroy the Acadians' homes and crops to discourage them from returning.

The captured Islanders were crowded aboard ships and sent to France. Historian Earle Lockerby has disproved the notion that the Island Acadians were forced into overcrowded, decrepit vessels that were not fit for the voyage. By the standards of the day, the ships were acceptable.

Lieutenant Colonel Andrew Rollo

Nevertheless, the Acadians suffered from sickness and disease engendered by the cramped, unsanitary conditions and unpalatable food. Approximately seven hundred Acadians who embarked from Havre-Saint-Pierre on the *Duke William* and the *Violet* in November and December 1758 perished at sea on their way to France. A violent Atlantic storm damaged both ships, and before the men on board the *Duke William* could aid their sister vessel, a squall separated them and all four hundred passengers on the *Violet* drowned. A similar fate befell the *Duke William*. The captain kept the ship afloat by filling liquor casks with air and placing them below deck. Just before the *Duke William* sank, four Acadians discovered a small boat onboard and escaped. They were the only Acadian survivors.

Mortality rates on the ships varied between ten and forty-five percent, depending on the vessel. One ship arrived in England after burying two hundred and fifty Acadians at sea, most of whom were children. The majority of its passengers were reported to be starving and almost naked. Many Acadians who reached Europe were later hospitalized and died from diseases they contracted aboard the ships.

The Acadians who arrived safely in France faced further difficulties. Most of them had never been to France, where the language and food differed from what they knew. They had to start life anew in a strange country. For years they had struggled to plant crops and build homes. Now all their hard work was either destroyed or in the hands of the hated British. In 1785, seven boatloads of Acadians left France for the Spanish colony of Louisiana to join the several hundred Acadians who had settled there in 1764. Today, Louisiana is home to more than one million descendants of these Acadians, whose name was subsequently shortened from the French *"Acadien"* to "Cadien" to "Cajun." During the twenty-five years following the 1763 treaty that ended the war, some Acadians returned to Acadia. Others remained in France or resettled in French Guyana or the Falkland Islands (Malvina Islands). Only two families, the Doirons and the Longuépées, returned to Île Saint-Jean.

Between 1,100 and 1,600 Islanders, including more than thirty families from Malpeque Bay, escaped the Deportation. Some successfully hid on the Island, but the majority went to the mainland. Some of these refugees eventually returned to the Island; the rest either remained on the mainland, went to such French colonies as the Magdalen Islands and Saint-Pierre and Miquelon, or sailed to Louisiana after the war ended.

On October 7, 1763, the Seven Years' War officially ended and North America became a British possession. At Fort Amherst, which was built on the site of Port-la-Joye, the British flag was raised. Île Saint-Jean was renamed St. John's Island. France would no longer play a major role in Canada's evolution. In the future, the Maritime colonies would be populated largely by non-French-speaking people.

ACADIAN FAMILY NAMES

The Deportation caused the extinction of at least twenty-four of the original Acadian and French families on the Island. Some Acadians later Anglicized their names: Aucoin became Wedge, Poirier became Perry, Pitre became Peters, and Bourque became Burke. About nine of every ten Acadians on Prince Edward Island today are descended from the families listed in the 1798 census: Arsenault, Doucet, Gaudet, Buote, Poirier, Pineau, Pitre, Landry, Longuépée, Aucoin, Chiasson, Gauthier, Martin, Richard, Cheverie, DesRoches, Blanchard, Gallant, Le Clerc, Bernard, Doiron, Bourque, Blaquière, Michel, Muise, St-Jean, Roussel, Downing, Gautreau, and Le Brun.

THE EVOLUTION OF FORT AMHERST/ PORT-LA-JOYE

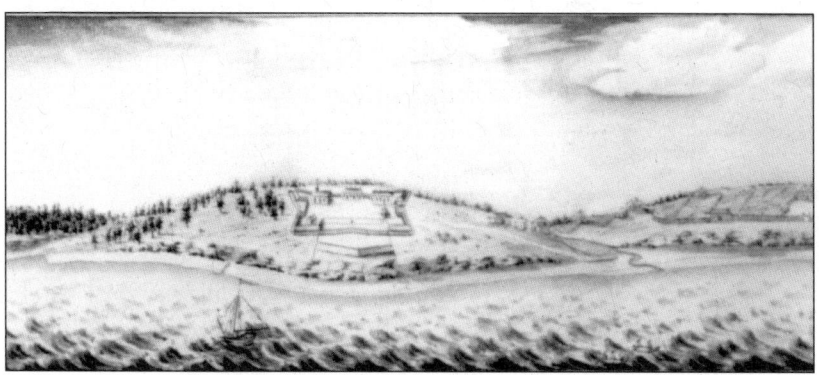

A 1734 design for a fort at Port-la-Joye

When the Compagnie de l'Île Saint-Jean arrived in Port-la-Joye in 1720, the men erected a chapel, storehouse, bakery, forge, powder magazine, barracks, and the commandant's lodgings, and cleared the site to have an unobstructed view of the harbour channel.

In the fall of 1744, the troops at Port-la-Joye abandoned the garrison and relocated to Louisbourg to help strengthen its defenses. The Acadians moved inland when the capital came under British rule the following year. The French garrison returned to Port-la-Joye in 1748, and rebuilt the fort, which had been destroyed by the British soldiers.

In 1758, Lord Rollo erected Fort Amherst on the same bluff as the French outpost had stood. With the return of peace in 1763, Fort Amherst's importance as a military fort declined and it soon fell into disrepair. Fifteen years later, the garrison was withdrawn from the fort, which was then abandoned, and a blockhouse and battery were constructed at the entrance of the harbour to protect Charlotte Town (as it was spelled prior to 1855) from French and American privateers during the Napoleonic Wars.

The Historic Sites and Monuments Board of Canada officially recognized Fort Amherst/Port-la-Joye as being of national historic significance in 1958. The site was commemorated for its role as the Island's seat of government from 1720 to 1770, as a port of entry for French and British settlers, and as an early colonial outpost. The site became a national historic park in 1967.

Today, the earthworks of Fort Amherst are still prominent and the area around the fort is cleared, much as it was in the mid-eighteenth century. The rolling grasslands and mixed woodland around the fort overlook the narrow channel entrance to Charlottetown Harbour.

After the peace treaty, several Acadian families returned to the Island to work for English fishing companies that recruited Acadians. However, the living conditions for the Acadians who came to the Island were dreadful. In 1765, British surveyor Samuel Holland reported on the Acadians' plight:

> *There are about thirty Acadian families on the island, who are regarded as prisoners, and kept on the same footing as those at Halifax. They are extremely poor, and maintain themselves by their industry in gardening, fishing, fowling, &c. The few remaining houses in the different parts of the island are very bad, and the quantity of cattle is but very inconsiderable.*

The Acadians' continued survival would depend on their own perseverance and British goodwill. By 1768, most Acadians resided in Malpeque, Rustico, Tracadie, St. Peters Harbour, and Bay Fortune.

CHAPTER FIVE

A British Colony

Once Great Britain gained control of St. John's Island, it faced the problem of deciding what to do with it. There was good fishing in the area, but no one knew how valuable its other resources were. Many people in Great Britain were willing to gamble that the Island was valuable, and almost as soon as the ink was dry on the 1763 peace treaty, King George III was flooded with requests for land.

In December 1763, John Perceval, Earl of Egmont, submitted an intriguing proposal to the king that had the support of many influential men in Great Britain, including the future governor of the Island, Walter Patterson. Egmont asked the king for the entire Island, plus a portion of Dominica in the West Indies. In return, he promised to divide the Island into fifty equal sections, forty of which would be given to important men who would be called lords, each of whom would pay Egmont a yearly rent. These lords would divide their land into twenty manors of two thousand acres each, and the manor lords would further divide the land. According to Egmont's plan, the Island would have one county town, forty market towns, and four hundred villages. The earl also promised to build a large castle, protected by cannons, to serve as a place of retreat and rendezvous for the settlers.

SCALPED AND MURDERED

A footnote attached to Lord Egmont's proposal indicates how ill-informed people in Britain were of the geography, climate, and peoples of their North American colonies. He wrote,

[T]he vast, impervious, and dangerous forests of America, intersected with seas, bays, lakes, rivers, marshes, and mountains; without roads, without inns or accommodations, locked up for half the year by snow and intense frost, and where the settler can scarce straggle from his habitation five hundred yards, even in times of peace, without risk of being intercepted, scalped, and murdered.

Surveying the Land

King George decided to learn more about his new colonies in North America before making any decisions as to what should be done with the land, and in 1764 he appointed Captain Samuel Johannes Holland to survey St. John's Island, Cape Breton, and the Magdalen Islands. Captain Holland was well suited to the task; a military engineer and skilled cartographer, in 1758 Holland had surveyed Louisbourg and prepared plans for its capture, which had earned him commendations for bravery and technical competence. Later, he had worked with James Cook to chart the St. Lawrence River in preparation for Britain's attack on Quebec City in 1759, and had subsequently been wounded in the siege of Quebec.

Captain Samuel Johannes Holland. While Holland was surveying the Island, his companion, Marie Josephte, bore him a son. John Frederick Holland was probably the first British baby born on St. John's Island.

Captain Holland arrived on St. John's Island in October 1764 and was immediately taken aback by his rudimentary accommodations. "I am obliged to build winter quarters for myself," he wrote. "I fear that it will not be too comfortable."

Holland divided his men into groups of five to survey the Island. Although the men loaded their toboggans with warm coats and blankets, the harsh winter conditions still left several men with frost-bitten extremities. Using astronomical observations, Holland divided the Island into sixty-seven lots or townships of about twenty thousand acres each, three counties (Kings, Queens, and Prince) of about five hundred thousand acres each, and fourteen parishes of approximately a hundred thousand acres each. Holland chose the sites of future towns, including the capital, which he named Charlotte Town in honour of King George III's wife, and provided a detailed account of the Island's forests, plants, soils, rivers, harbours, and climate. His map formed the basis of the present division of land on Prince Edward Island.

Giving the Island Away: The Lottery

On July 23, 1767, the British government rewarded many of those who had played a significant role in the Seven Years' War with a piece of St. John's Island. The applicants had been interviewed and had written letters explaining why they deserved consideration. The government selected about a hundred of these applicants to take part in a land lottery. On the day of the lottery, each person's name was written on a slip of paper and placed in a box. The first name picked received Lot 1, the second name chosen received Lot 2, and this continued until sixty-four of the sixty-seven lots had been granted. Approximately 1.4 million acres were given away on a single day.

For most grants, the Crown reserved a five-hundred-foot-wide belt of land above the high-water mark to support the fishery. It also retained Lot 66, and reserved land for schools and churches, as well as for the county capitals of Georgetown, Charlotte Town, and Princetown (now called Summerside). Lots 40 and 59 had been granted prior to the lottery to merchants who had long been interested in the colony. The British government awarded Samuel Holland for his work surveying the Island by adding his name to the lottery, in which he received Lot 28. Lord Egmont was offered an entire parish, but he turned it down as insufficient for his plans.

The British government required the new landowners to pay for the construction of roads and jails and provide salaries for judges,

CAPTAIN HOLLAND'S DESCRIPTION OF THE ISLAND

In 1765, Holland described the Island's flora and fauna and provided his reasons for selecting the colony's major town sites:

In most parts of the island the Sarsaparilla Root is in great abundance, and very good. The Mountain Shrub and Maiden Hair are also pretty common, of whose leaves and berries the Acadian settlers frequently make a kind of tea. The ground is in general covered with strawberries and cranberries, in their different seasons, which are very good.... Port la Joie, Cardigan and Richmond Bays are without dispute the only places where ships of burthen can safely enter, and consequently most proper to erect the principal towns and settlements upon.

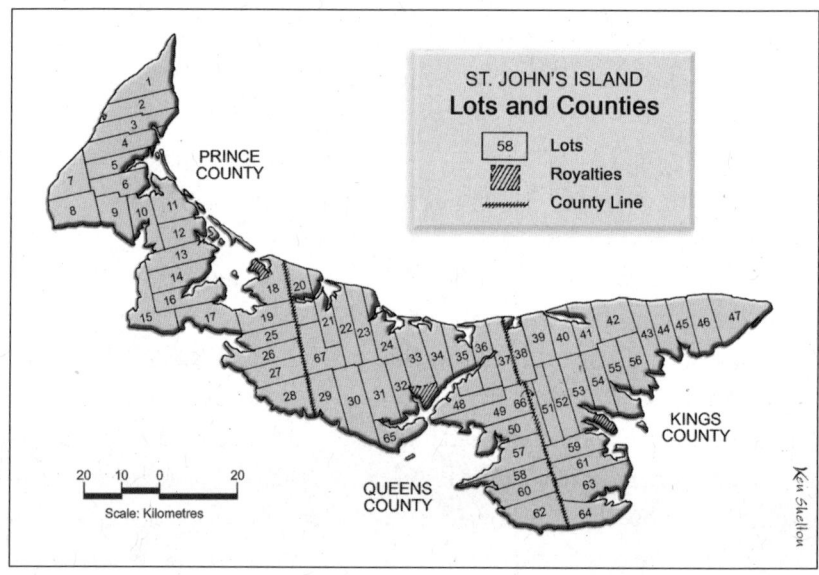

The lots and counties of St. John's Island as they were divided in 1767

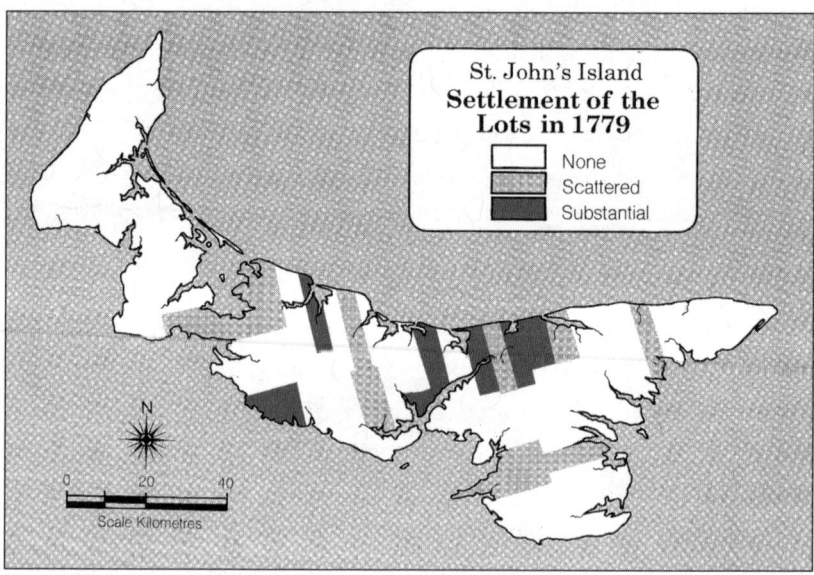

The settled lots on St. John's Island, 1779. Immigration was agonizingly slow on the Island. From 1770 to 1775, only about one thousand people came to the Island. Two decades later, one-third of the Island's sixty-seven lots were still without settlers.

sheriffs, and government leaders through a small annual fee called a "quit rent"—the more valuable the land, the higher the quit rent. The owners were also obligated to settle, within ten years, one Protestant person from outside of Great Britain for every 110 acres they had been allotted. Roman Catholics were not desired as settlers because the British government distrusted them—especially after the recent wars with Catholic France. If the landowners did not fulfill these terms, the government reserved the right to repossess the land.

Very few owners actually paid their quit rents to the government or brought over the required number of settlers. Most of the lottery winners had asked for the land solely for speculative purposes. As a result, after ten years, about one-quarter of the lots had been sold at least once, but few settlers had been brought to the Island.

THOMAS CURTIS: STRANGER IN A STRANGE LAND

The first immigrants to St. John's Island faced unimaginable difficulties. The voyage across the Atlantic often tested the endurance of the hardiest passengers. Most emigrants could not afford separate cabins and were crowded below deck in steerage, where bunk beds were stacked two or three high. Four people, sometimes complete strangers, often shared a two-metre-square bunk. These people spent up to six weeks below deck, where there were no windows, toilets, or privacy. Amidst foul air, dirty water, rancid food, and open cooking fires, sick people lay moaning in their beds, babies were born, and people died. While some vessels sailed peacefully across the Atlantic, others encountered nothing but trouble.

Thomas Curtis's ship, the *Elizabeth*, was in the latter category. Curtis was a British immigrant who sailed from London to St. John's Island in 1775 in search of a better life. He later returned to England and wrote a long account of his experiences. According to Curtis's recollections, Robert Clark, who owned Lots 21 and 49 on the Island, had told him about the excellent timber stands, the high wages for labourers, the rivers that "abounded with fish," and the abundance of such game as deer and turkeys that awaited him on the Island.

The *Elizabeth* set sail on August 8, 1775. For the first three days of the voyage, Curtis was so seasick that he didn't leave his bed. As a steerage passenger, he relied on candles for light, salt water for bathing, and pails for defecation. His meals consisted of salt beef and pork, and pudding twice a week. When the ship neared Newfoundland, the passengers caught cod and halibut, which they cooked in a large iron pot with slices of pork fat. This dish, Curtis wrote, was called "chowder."

On November 5, one of the men on the ship called out "land on the lee bow." The wind was blowing hard and everyone feared for their lives as the gale blew the vessel toward shore. The crew dropped the anchors and cut down the masts, but the ship continued to drift closer to the breakers. Ultimately, the ship drifted over four sandbars before running aground near Cavendish Inlet. The passengers took the lifeboats to shore, where they started a fire and gave thanks for their survival.

At the time of the *Elizabeth*'s arrival, the Island's population was less than 1,300 and about a quarter of these people had arrived in the previous five years. Most of the settlements were on the north shore of the Island and thus Curtis had seen nothing but forests from the ship. Gathered around the fire, Curtis wrote that he and the other passengers were "still in want of many things to make [them] comfortable," and lamented that there was "no chair nor Table no bed Nothing to Eat no house to cover [them]." Their hastily constructed shelter leaked and everyone spent the night standing around the fire in the rain. The wind blew sparks on them, which burned their clothes and skin.

The rain continued into the second night and the wind blew the settlers' shelter down. By morning, everyone was complaining of hunger, and Curtis imagined such horrors as eating their dogs or throwing dice to see who would be eaten first. The next morning, however, the storm subsided and the men made their way to the *Elizabeth* and rescued several casks of oatmeal, rum, and bacon. The casks of oatmeal were soggy and full of sand, but everyone was so hungry that they dipped their heads into the barrels and "ate more like pigs than men." Later, the women cooked oatmeal cakes. Curtis wrote that his oatmeal cake was "the Sweetest morsel [he] ever Ate in [his] life though the Outside was burnt black the middle was not half done." On the ninth day after the settlers' arrival on the Island, a boat arrived with provisions. They were saved.

When Thomas Curtis finally arrived at a settlement (New London), he was repulsed by its diminutive size and log houses. "I then began to repent of my Voyage and wish my Selfe in Old London again," he wrote. Since it was too late in the season for ships to return to Britain, he stayed the winter. The final words in his account were: "I cant express The Joy I Felt when I got on my native Country the 2d of Feb. 1777."

First Settlements

Although most of the landlords quickly lost interest in the Island, between 1767 and the beginning of the American Revolution in 1775 several owners attempted to colonize their lands. Sir James Montgomery founded settlements at Covehead and Stanhope; Robert Stewart sent about eighty Scottish settlers to Malpeque; Captain John MacDonald established colonies at Tracadie and Scotchfort; Robert Clark and Robert Campbell brought approximately two hundred colonists to New London; Captain Holland sponsored a few families at Cape Traverse; and Thomas DesBrisay helped two hundred people settle in Lots 31 and 33. Although the landlords had promised to only settle Protestants recruited from outside Great Britain, the majority of the immigrants were Scottish Roman Catholics. The rest were mostly English and Scottish Protestants.

The British government generally ignored St. John's Island in favour of its other North American possessions, and few settlers wished to rent land on the Island when they could purchase their own farms quite cheaply in other British colonies. As a result, the Island generally attracted only the poorer and less-educated immigrants.

Many of the early settlers came in groups under the auspices of one of the large landowners. James Montgomery, for example, was an important politician and businessman in Scotland who arranged for the settlement of his land on Lot 34. In 1769, Montgomery became interested in establishing a flax farm on the Island and hired David Lawson, a British farmer familiar with flax farming, to oversee his farm in return for half the profits after seven years' service. The farm work was to be performed by servants, who agreed to stay for four years, after which time Montgomery promised to rent them land at inexpensive rates.

Having recruited about fifty indentured servants in Perthshire, Scotland, Lawson set sail with his family on the *Falmouth* on April 8, 1770. After a long and difficult voyage, the *Falmouth* reached Covehead Bay on June 1. Expecting "better provisions than oatmeal and salt water," the settlers were shocked by the primitive conditions. Eventually, a shipload of food arrived from Three Rivers.

Over the next four years, Lawson and the other colonists gradually cleared the land, planted seeds, and built a grain mill. However, the farm, which was called Stanhope after Montgomery's Scottish estate, suffered numerous misfortunes. The mill was twice destroyed by fire and once by a flood. One worker was crushed by a large pine tree that he was chopping down. Two men drowned. Finally, just when the flax farm began to make money, the workers' contracts expired and they scattered across the Island. With the outbreak of the American Revolution in 1775, Montgomery turned his attention elsewhere. Lawson decided to remain on the Island and sat in the House of Assembly between 1773 and 1785.

Captain John MacDonald's reasons for settling the Tracadie area (Lot 36) were quite different from Montgomery's motives for settling his own lot. In 1746, after England defeated the Scottish clans at the Battle of Culloden, the British government adopted a series of repressive measures to crush Scottish culture. Consequently, the Protestant owner of South Uist, an island in the Hebrides, threatened to expel any Catholic tenants who refused to renounce their Roman Catholic faith, and also hired a teacher to proselytize their children. When other islands in the Hebrides adopted similar practices, the Catholic bishops in Scotland sought a way to end this religious persecution. Captain MacDonald, the 8th Laird of Glenaladale, agreed to help the bishops resettle "these destitute people," and sent his brother Donald to America to find a suitable location. Favourable rumours about James Montgomery's flax farm in Tracadie, as well as exaggerated stories about its rich soil and mild climate, convinced MacDonald to purchase Lot 36 from Montgomery. With the assistance of the Catholic Church, MacDonald recruited Catholic tenants from South Uist and elsewhere.

Since the Protestant landowners in the Hebrides did not want to lose their tenants, they spread rumours that anyone who went to the Island would be sold into slavery. Partly as a result, only 210 settlers disembarked from the *Alexander* at Scotchfort in 1772. Donald MacDonald, Captain MacDonald's brother, took charge of the colony while Captain John, as he was called, remained in Scotland to raise money and recruit more people. Upon their arrival, the Scottish settlers were unhappy and "unnerved" by the wilderness conditions they encountered. One Catholic priest wrote of the conditions: "There is no money, no clothes, and no meat unless we pay four times what it is worth. It breaks my heart that my poor friends who were doing well before they left Scotland are now upon the brink of great misery and poverty." The following year, Captain John arrived with more colonists and supplies, and the colony survived.

The MacDonald brothers left the Island in 1775 to fight in the American Revolution. Donald was killed in battle in 1781 and John did not return until 1792. During John's sixteen-year absence, his sister Nelly managed his estate. In addition to ensuring that the crops were planted and harvested and the ninety head of cattle were fed, Nelly attempted to collect rent from the tenants, who had little cash and few markets for their produce. She also supervised the construction of a house for her brother according to his specifications. When Captain John returned to the Island, he brought a new wife, Margaret, who took over the management of the estate when John was absent. Captain John MacDonald died in 1810 on his estate in Tracadie. After his death, the colonists remained on the land and the settlement continued to grow.

Selkirk's Settlers

The largest group of Scottish settlers came to the Island under the auspices of Thomas Douglas. As a young man, Douglas had travelled through the Highlands of Scotland, where the landowners had displaced many residents for sheep farming. He was shocked by how wretched these displaced people were, and wished to help them. As the seventh son of the earl of Selkirk, Douglas stood little chance of inheriting the family's fortune. However, due to a series of unfortunate deaths, he became the 5th Earl of Selkirk in 1799, after which he had the time and the finances to pursue his dreams.

In 1799, Douglas turned his attention to the Hebrides, particularly the Isle of Skye, where unemployment was high and the crops had been poor for several years. He arranged for the residents of the Isle

Thomas Douglas, the 5th Earl of Selkirk

of Skye to resettle in Sault Ste. Marie, Upper Canada, but when the British government withdrew its support for his plans, Selkirk bought eighty thousand acres of land on Prince Edward Island (the newly renamed St. John's Island). In July 1803, Selkirk and about eight hundred Highlanders set sail for the Orwell–Point Prim area aboard the *Polly*, the *Dykes*, and the *Oughton*.

Although Selkirk's settlers experienced similar problems to those that plagued earlier immigrants, the settlement prospered, partly because Selkirk treated his people well. He kept them together so they could preserve their traditional values and customs and assist one another. He also agreed to sell the settlers the land rather than rent it. Equally important, the Highlanders who came with Selkirk had been among the more prosperous tenant farmers in Scotland and were thus better equipped to survive.

Selkirk remained on the Island only a few months, and his subsequent contact with the settlers on the Island was unsatisfactory. His Island agent did not keep him informed of the colony's progress and sold the valuable timber on the property without approval. Selkirk gradually lost interest in the Island and turned his attention to establishing the Red River colony near present-day Winnipeg. His settlers remained in the area and prospered.

Loyalists and the American Revolution

The American Revolution (1775–1783) was one of the most important events in Canadian history. It divided Great Britain's possessions in North America into the United States of America in the south and British North America in the north. Whereas the northern colonies had previously been of little consequence to Great Britain compared

Loyalist refugees departing Boston for Nova Scotia

to the more profitable Thirteen Colonies (which eventually formed the United States), they now assumed greater prominence.

The American Revolution pitted brother against brother, friend against friend, and husband against wife. The Patriots, who wanted the Thirteen Colonies to become independent of Great Britain, often persecuted the Loyalists, who were loyal to the British crown, for their beliefs. In several colonies the Loyalists were stripped of their right to vote, thrown in prison, fired from their jobs, run out of town, or had their property confiscated. Life remained unbearable for the Loyalists after the war, and many of them relocated to British territory, where people were sympathetic to their cause. Most returned to England or went to the British West Indies, Bermuda, Belize, or Florida. About fifty thousand fled north to Quebec, Nova Scotia, and St. John's Island, doubling the population of the Maritime region. This was the first mass movement of political refugees in modern history.

Kidnapped from Charlotte Town

Shortly after the Thirteen Colonies declared their independence from Great Britain in 1775, George Washington, the commander-in-chief of the Continental Armed Forces, sent two armed vessels to the St.

Lawrence River to intercept several ships sent from England to Quebec with arms and provisions for the British troops. The captains were allowed to take one-third of the value of any prizes they captured, but were to treat Canadian vessels "with all kindness, and by no means suffer them to be injured or molested."

The two American ships captured several vessels, but never reached the St. Lawrence. Instead, on November 17, 1775, the warships appeared in Charlotte Town harbour. When the Island's acting governor, Phillips Callbeck, met them in the harbour, he was kidnapped and held captive aboard one of their ships. The raiders then carried away Callbeck's entire stock of provisions, which were meant to provide for his and other families during the winter. They also ransacked Callbeck's house, taking curtains, bedding, jewellery, carpets, plates, alcohol, food, and the Island's silver seal—leaving him "without a single glass of wine, without a candle to burn, bread to eat, nor clothes to wear." After reading the family's correspondence, the Americans searched for Callbeck's wife, Elizabeth, to "cut her throat" because her father was a Loyalist supporter, but Elizabeth was safe at their farm in the country. Next, according to Callbeck, "these brutal violators of domestic felicity" broke into Governor Walter Patterson's empty house and took what they wanted. Finally, the raiders forced surveyor general Thomas Wright and naval officer David Higgins aboard ship and returned to the Thirteen Colonies with the three kidnapped men.

The affair ended happily for Callbeck, Higgins, and Wright. When the ships landed near Boston, George Washington apologized "very politely and allowed them to return to Halifax on a foul-smelling vessel," according to Callbeck. Washington reported that the American captains had acted without his consent and later dismissed them from their commands.

INSULTING LANGUAGE

Upon his return to the Island, Phillips Callbeck wrote a detailed report about the American attack on Charlottetown. At one point in the report, his feelings about his captors become very evident: "After they had accomplished thus far of their cruelty, they made Mr. Wright a prisoner, and, with insulting language, laughed at the tears of his wife and sister, who were in the greatest agony of distress at so cruel a separation from their husband and brother."

Upon his return to the Island in May 1776, Phillips Callbeck threw his energy into improving the Island's defences. As a result of Callbeck's efforts, Britain sent a warship to Charlotte Town; ordered its fleet to be more diligent in protecting the area; sent troops and ammunition to the Island; and had a seven-gun battery constructed near Charlotte Town to protect the harbour. Due to these precautions, except for small raids at St. Peter's and Georgetown, the Island escaped further attacks.

Slavery on the Island
In 1781, under British possession, the Island government passed the following law legalizing slavery:

> *1. That all Slaves, whether Negroes or Mulattoes, residing at present on this Island, or that may hereafter be imported or brought therein, shall be deemed slaves, notwithstanding his, her or their Conversion to Christianity; nor shall the act of Baptism performed on any such Negro or Mulatto alter his, her or their condition.*

> *2. And be it further enacted, That all Negro and Mulatto Servants who are now on this Island, or many hereafter be imported or brought therein (being Slaves), shall continue such, unless freed by his, her or their respective Owners.*

> *3. And be it further enacted by the authority aforesaid, That all children born of Women Slaves shall belong to and be the property of the Master or Mistresses of such Slaves.*

Historian Jim Hornby has conjectured that the purpose of this legislation was to encourage Loyalists, many of whom came north with their black slaves, to settle in Saint John's Island. The Island's elite, including the governor, the chief justice, the attorney general, the speaker of the house, and the colonial treasurer, all kept slaves. Although the Island's Supreme Court affirmed the validity of slave sales in 1802, slave holding, which was not very profitable, gradually declined. In 1825 it was officially abolished. Thereafter, the majority of the Island's black residents lived near Cardigan or in a section of Charlotte Town that became known as "The Bog." The majority of the Island's present black community is descended from David and Kesiah (Wilson) Shepard, two of the four slaves Loyalist Edmund Fanning brought with him to the Island.

Loyalist Settlers
Encouraged by the Island landlords' promises of free land in return for clearing the forests and building roads, approximately five hundred Loyalists settled on the Island in Bedeque, Orwell, Tryon, Vernon River, and East Point. However, when they discovered that the landlords had no intention of keeping their promises and that much of the land given to them was on disputed property, several hundred Loyalists left the Island for the mainland. Those who remained represented a cross-section of late-eighteenth century society—farmers, fishers, and tradesmen, as well as merchants and professionals. One Loyalist, Edmund Fanning, served as the Island's second lieutenant-governor from 1786 to 1805.

Irish Settlers
Unlike the Scottish settlers, most Irish immigrants were not recruited to come to the Island. Still, according to calculations by historian Brendan O'Grady, by 1798 Irish settlers constituted about ten percent of the Island's population. Some Irish immigrants initially went to Newfoundland before sailing for the Island. Early in the nineteenth century, Newfoundland deported its unemployed citizens to the Island, where there was a demand for winter labourers. However, when Newfoundland commenced sending its criminals to the Island, the government passed a law to prohibit this practice.

The largest group of Irish immigrants came to escape the harsh conditions at home in the period from 1830 to 1850. Most arrived in

Charlotte Town, where they constituted forty percent of the population by 1850, before gradually migrating to virtually every township on the Island. Unlike the case in most other British North American colonies, few of the Irish people on the Island were refugees from the Irish Potato Famine of the mid-1840s.

POPULATION GROWTH, 1798-1855

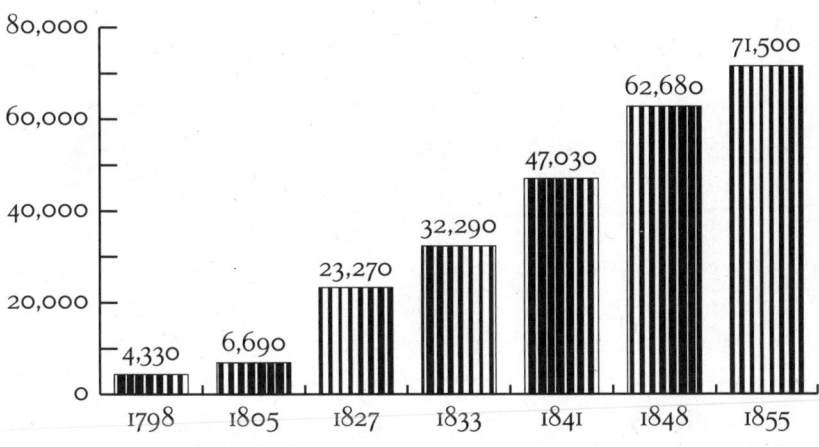

The Acadians Start Over

For several years, the Island Acadians who had escaped the Deportation lived in fear of being forcibly removed from the Island. In 1764, Samuel Holland described them as living in "little cabins or huts in the woods" and subsisting "on the fish they have cured in the summer, and game which they frequently kill, as hares and partridges, lynxes or wild cats, otters, martins, or musk rats, -- none of which they refuse to eat, as necessity presses them."

The Acadian communities clung to their traditions and resisted assimilation. Physically, most Acadians lived apart from the other Island inhabitants and retained their traditional dress, which further isolated them from mainstream society. Another tradition they kept alive was the Twelfth Night celebration, which marked the coming of the Epiphany, when everyone gathered together on the night of January 6 and shared a cake with two favours baked into it. The male and female who discovered the favours in their pieces of cake were crowned king and queen for the evening. Another tradition the Acadians retained was Candlemas; on February 2, the young men went door to door to collect food for the poor. Two favourite Acadian dishes were *fricot* (potato soup with chicken) and *pâté* (meat pie made with pork and chicken or rabbit).

Occasionally, British merchants hired the Acadians as fishers or boat-builders and paid them with clothing, rum, flour, or ammunition. But as the numbers of British immigrants increased, the Acadians were forced to give up the land they had cleared and move elsewhere. No sooner would they clear this new land than they would be evicted again.

By 1798, Acadians comprised only fifteen percent of the population and were concentrated in Malpeque Bay, Rustico, and Bay Fortune. Problems with the landowners soon forced the Acadians in Malpeque Bay to move to Tignish and then to Cascumpec, Egmont Bay, Mont-Carmel, and Miscouche. Some Acadians from Bay Fortune moved to Rollo Bay, while others settled in Cape Breton. The Acadian presences at St. Peters Bay and Tracadie completely disappeared.

Moved by guilt, in 1852 the Island government allowed Acadians to buy the land in Lot 15 at a reduced rate. Today, Lot 15 has the most homogeneous Acadian population in the province and is the area where the French language has been best preserved.

The Oldest Islanders: The Mi'kmaq

The British government was not as friendly towards the Mi'kmaq as the French authorities had been. Many Mi'kmaq had converted to Catholicism and had been French allies. At the end of the Seven Years' War, the British government gave small amounts of land to the Mi'kmaq in New Brunswick and Nova Scotia; however, on Prince Edward Island, all the land was given away to wealthy British proprietors.

To most settlers and government officials, the Mi'kmaq were all but invisible. After two years of gathering information about the

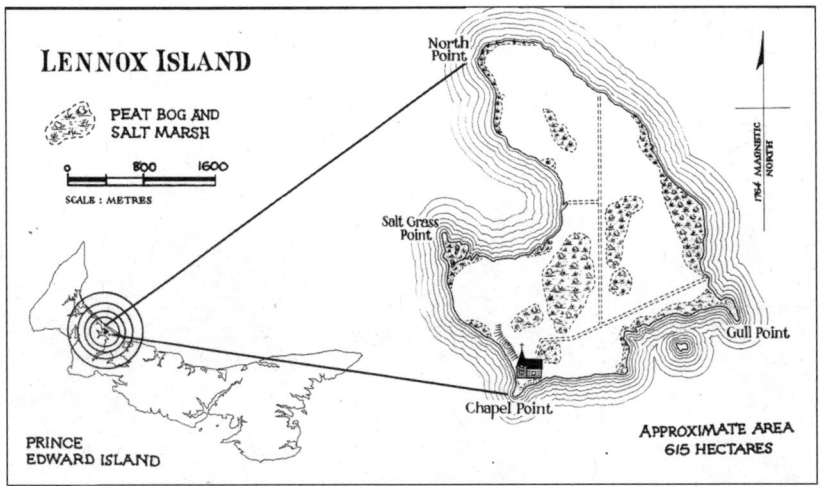

A map of Lennox Island, 1764

Island, Governor Walter Patterson reported in 1772 that there were "no Natives, or Indians, who either inhabit, or claim any right to" the Island, thus indicating the absence of contact with the surviving Mi'kmaq.

For several decades after Britain gained control of the Island, the Mi'kmaq continued to roam the Island in search of game, but as the settlers cleared the forests and erected fences, the wild animals that the Mi'kmaq relied on to survive slowly disappeared. When the settlement of the land made it difficult to move about the Island freely, the Mi'kmaq asked the government for land of their own, but the government was unwilling to help. Finally, Sir James Montgomery, a wealthy British landlord, offered to let them live rent-free on Lennox Island, and in 1856, Charles Worrell, who owned most of Lots 38 to 42, donated 204 acres in Morell to several Aboriginal families.

Roman Catholic missionary Abbé de Callone persuaded several Mi'kmaq families to settle year-round on Lennox Island, where they built a chapel, cleared several hectares of land, and planted potatoes. Unfortunately, one-third of Lennox Island was swampy and was therefore unfit for habitation. Moreover, settlers came to Lennox Island to cut timber and gather wild hay in the marshes to feed their livestock, depleting the island's supply. Despite Mi'kmaq complaints,

A Mi'kmaq family on Lennox Island

Montgomery rented the marshland to the settlers rather than to the Mi'kmaq, who could not pay for it.

In 1856, the first Aboriginal census listed 309 Mi'kmaq inhabitants. It was difficult to determine the exact number of Mi'kmaq because few remained in the same location for long, as hunting and fishing required them to move from place to place. Only a handful of families lived year-round on Lennox Island. The Island Mi'kmaq hunted, fished, and earned meager incomes selling firewood and handcrafted goods. The men fashioned barrels, furniture, brooms, axe handles, toy bows and arrows, snowshoes, and canoes. The women made beautiful beaded cloth goods, boxes with porcupine quillwork mosaics, and birchbark utensils embroidered with animal hair. Woodsplint baskets, which were made by the entire family, were also popular items. When all else failed, the Mi'kmaq were forced to beg to survive.

Mi'kmaq Advocates

Uneducated, illiterate in English, and denied the right to vote, the Island's Mi'kmaq had to rely on others to improve their lot in life.

Thomas Irwin was a passionate advocate of Mi'kmaq rights. Irwin, a Roman Catholic who was born in Ireland and had been forced to learn English, came to Prince Edward, where he earned his teaching certificate and practised surveying. Irwin was also an accomplished student of languages. It was while he was learning the Mi'kmaq language that Irwin identified with their plight. Like him, the Mi'kmaq had been oppressed by the English, evicted from their lands, and threatened with the loss of their identity and language.

Irwin wrote a three-hundred-page book on "the principles of the Mickmack language" in 1830. The next year, he unsuccessfully petitioned the government to provide education and land for the Mi'kmaq. For the next seventeen years, Irwin remained the only white person on the Island to demonstrate public sympathy for the Mi'kmaq.

In 1846, a Baptist minister named Silas Rand arrived in Charlotte Town. Rand also compiled an English–Mi'kmaq dictionary and unsuccessfully petitioned the government to help the Mi'kmaq. In 1850, he wrote in the *Christian Messenger*, "I can scarcely suppress a feeling of shame that I am a white man—since our coloured brethren have been so unjustly and unmercifully treated by us, because forsooth, like ourselves, they have the audacity to wear the skin which the great Creator gave them." Unfortunately, this appeal went unheeded.

Finally, in 1854, the government appointed a commissioner to supervise and help the Mi'kmaq earn a living. Eleven years later, the Island's Indian commissioner, Theophilus Stewart, attended a meeting of the Aborigines Protection Society in London, England. Although this society was dedicated to helping Aboriginal groups around the world, it had generally ignored the Aboriginal Peoples in the Maritimes. Stewart's visit changed its priorities and in 1870 the Aborigines Protection Society purchased Lennox Island as a reserve for the Mi'kmaq. Three years later, the federal government assumed all responsibility for the Mi'kmaq.

CHAPTER SIX
Pioneer Life

The settlers' first impression of the Island was often of the tall forests that presented an almost unbroken line of dense foliage that seemingly rose from the sea. One Gaelic settler wrote, "It is lonely here in Murray Harbour not knowing English.... No one can procure anything unless he wrests it from the forest. The length of winter is depressing; it is fully half one's lifetime.... You will not come to live here if you are in your right mind." As this opinion suggests, pioneer life on the Island was both physically and psychologically arduous.

Island Transportation
As late as 1821, the Island's population numbered only about fifteen thousand people, most of whom resided in small villages along the coast and had precarious links to the outside world. The only road that existed on the Island in 1791 joined Covehead and Charlotte Town. To solve this problem, the government compelled every male over the age of twenty-one to work eight hours on the roads at least four days each year.

The narrow dirt roads that the men laid across the Island wound past swamps, over streams, and around tangled roots. They were virtually impassable in the winter, when the strong winds created huge snowdrifts, and in the spring and fall, when the heavy red mud turned the rutted roads into knee-deep quagmires. Charlotte Town had a few four-wheeled carriages, but most travel was confined to foot or horse. In November 1861, Charlottetown doctor John Mackieson noted that a thirty-kilometre trip to New Glasgow took three and a half hours because the trail was "like walking through liquid mud."

In such primitive conditions the difference between life and death might depend upon how quickly a doctor could attend a patient. In 1834, for example, Dr. Mackieson was urgently called to St. Peter's

A Prince Edward Island stamp from 1861

to treat a case of strangulated hernia. It was a sixty-kilometre trip, and the physician did not arrive until late in the evening, forcing him to operate by candlelight. Six years later, Alexander Nicholson of Murray Harbour dislocated and severely gashed his leg in the woods. He suffered for several days before his wife could bring him to Charlotte Town. By then it was too late for Alexander, who died from his infected wounds, and almost too late for his wife, who delivered twins shortly after her arrival in town.

In 1775, Governor Patterson hired several men to transport the winter mail from the mainland to the Island by canoe. By thus reducing the Island's isolation, he hoped to encourage others to come and settle there. Initially, mail sent from Great Britain to the Island went to Halifax to be sorted. Since there were several places named St. John's, mail on its way to St. John's Island was easily lost. Mail from overseas was stored in Charlotte Town until someone came to collect it. Local newspapers alerted readers who had mail to be picked up by publishing a list of the unclaimed letters. In 1827, postal carriers began delivering the mail once a week to local post offices, and by 1855 there were about forty-eight post offices on the Island, most of which were located in private homes or general stores. Prince Edward Island issued its first postage stamp in 1861.

In 1827, a weekly winter ferry connected Cape Traverse, St. John's Island, and Cape Tormentine, New Brunswick. Permanent steamboat service to the mainland began fifteen years later when Prince Edward Island Steam Navigation Company commenced sending boats between Nova Scotia, Charlotte Town, Bedeque, Georgetown, and New Brunswick every two weeks. Although the Island was now less isolated, the service was expensive and the boats were never on time.

Men pulling iceboats across the frozen Northumberland Strait, 1906

In winter, Island residents used small iceboats to cross the Northumberland Strait. These boats were usually about five metres long and just over a metre wide, and were covered with tin to protect them from the ice. Depending upon the weather, the men used sails, oars, or paddles to cross the strait. When the ice became too thick, the men attached themselves to the iceboats with long leather harnesses and pulled the boats over the ice on metal runners. The rates to cross the strait via iceboat were two dollars for women, four dollars for men who wished to remain in the boat, and two dollars for men who helped pull the boat across the ice. In favourable conditions, a typical crossing took about three-and-a-half hours.

After an accident in 1885, in which several men attempting to cross the frozen strait were lost on the ice for two days and almost died, each boat was required to take a compass, two extra paddles, food, and the means to make a fire.

Early Farming Practices

The settlers' first years were a continuous struggle to survive. Trees needed to be cleared, houses had to be built, firewood cut, seeds

A sketch by Island artist Robert Harris depicting settlers gathering marsh hay for fodder

planted, livestock cared for, wheat threshed, furniture made, meals cooked, and children raised. It was backbreaking work. Farmers broadcast seeds by hand and harvested grain with scythes, gathered it with wooden rakes, and threshed it by beating it on the ground with flails. The first mechanical threshers, powered by a horse walking on a treadmill, appeared on the Island in 1828.

Settlers cleared the forests either by cutting down the trees and burning them or by girdling the larger trees of their bark and letting them die slowly. Since it took many years to clear the land completely of tree stumps, the first settlers planted their crops among the stumps. They planted potatoes in little mounds between the stumps in the burnt clearings, fertilized them with ashes, and covered them with earth until each clump resembled a small molehill. In 1771, Governor Patterson reported that the year's potato crop was a "phenomenal success," and by 1790, island farmers were exporting small quantities of potatoes to Nova Scotia and New Brunswick. In 1805, the average farm devoted fifteen percent of its acreage to potatoes. The thin red topsoil on the Island was also good for growing wheat, oats, flax, peas, turnips, hat, and barley. Farmers also raised sheep, cattle, pigs, and horses, which were fed marsh hay gathered from the numerous salt marshes on the Island.

By the middle of the nineteenth century, the Island's economy was based on the small family farm. Island crops were so plentiful that they were exported to Great Britain, Bermuda, and Nova Scotia and New Brunswick. Imports to the Island included tea, tobacco, nails, molasses, rum, sugar, and manufactured goods.

Much of the credit for the growth of the agriculture industry on the Island belonged to the many agricultural societies that were organized between 1825 and 1850. These societies encouraged farmers to use modern farming methods by organizing fairs to promote better agriculture techniques, giving scientific talks, and importing new grains and farm machinery. The societies also imported Clydesdale horses; Ayrshire, Shorthorn, Hereford, and Angus cattle; Leicester sheep; and Yorkshire, Berkshire, and Tomworth pigs to improve the quality of island livestock.

By the 1820s, farmers were beginning to rotate their crops in order to prevent the nutrient content of the soil from being depleted. Farmers also used fish, lobster shells, barnyard manure, smelt, capelin, and mussel mud to fertilize the soil and prevent it from becoming exhausted.

A MONOTONOUS DIET

The settlers' normal diet consisted of oatmeal porridge, potatoes, pickled herring, and cod, supplemented by wild berries, shellfish, ducks, and geese when they were in season. Thomas Curtis described the poor food situation in New London in the winter of 1775: "Having nothing now to Eat but Salt fish and potatoes for dinner we used to have hot and other times cold this kind of food three times a day, some of us soon grew tired of." Fifty-seven years later, John Lewellin, a British writer, noted in his emigration tract that "many of the Settlers live very much on Fish (herring, mackerel, cod, lobsters, &) and potatoes, oatmeal porridge and milk, but people generally are getting in to more expensive habits in food, dress, dwellings, and furniture," indicating that the quality of life on the Island was improving.

Early Homes and Clothing

The first homes on the Island were usually small log cabins made from newly cut trees. Since there was no ready supply of labourers, or the money to afford them, neighbours gathered for house-raising frolics to help new families erect their homes before winter. Everyone brought food and drinks and stayed after supper for singing and dancing.

After visiting the Island with the thought of settling there, Walter Johnstone described Island architecture in 1821 for the benefit of prospective settlers:

> *Their houses are all constructed of wood, some of squared, and others unsquared logs, laid horizontally, and dove-tailed at the corners. Others have [frame homes]: some are thatched with birch bark, others with boards; and the old settlers generally have them shingled....These houses are uncommonly hot in summer, and cold in winter, and soon begin to rot at the ground, if not underfooted with brick or stone.*

To keep out the cold, settlers stuffed the spaces between the round logs that made up the walls of their cabins with moss, mud, and wood chips. On cold winter evenings, they rolled a large log onto the fire to keep it burning all night. The fireplace provided them with warmth, light, and heat for cooking. Since the first friction matches did not appear until 1827, the settlers rarely allowed the fire to die in the winter—otherwise, flint and tinder was required to relight it. Islanders placed hot coals in metal containers to serve as foot and hand warmers and to warm the sheets before going to bed. Their bed warmers resembled frying pans with hinged lids and long wooden handles. In the morning, it was often so cold that the pioneers awakened to find that their breath had formed frost on the bed covers, and that the water in their bedside jugs had frozen.

Islanders lined their winter coats, cloaks, mittens, and leggings with fur to stay warm. In winter, the men wore wool flannel shirts to keep out the cold. The same cloth wicked away their sweat in the

A sketch of a typical Acadian home in Rustico by Robert Harris

summer. It was common for farmers, who had few clothes, to go for months without removing most of their clothing. Women preferred woollen dresses to cotton ones when they cooked in front of the open fireplace because wool caught fire less frequently. Cotton was also imported and therefore more expensive.

Women in Pioneer Society

The tasks that typically fell to women in pioneer society, including the preparation of food and the creation of such necessities as clothing, soap, medicines, and candles, required considerable skill. Even well-to-do women were expected to have mastered the domestic arts so that they could instruct their servants in these skills.

Women's social standing and wealth were inescapably tied to their husbands'. Outside the home, there were few jobs open to females. Women were not allowed to vote or run for political office, or to be ministers, lawyers, or doctors. The legal system also catered to men. Women could not sue, enter into contracts, or acquire or dispose of property. The family's money was controlled by the man of the house, including any income earned by female family members. Fathers had sole legal control over their children. Prior to 1840, grounds for divorce were limited to adultery. Changes in the divorce law in the 1860s established a double standard in which husbands could gain divorce on the sole grounds of adultery, whereas wives had to demonstrate that their husbands had been guilty of adultery coupled with either desertion for a period of two years, sodomy, bigamy, rape, or bestiality. Perhaps due to these strict regulations, in 1901 there were only five divorced men and nine divorced women in the province, and the Island was the only jurisdiction in British North America that did not grant a single divorce in the last three decades of the nineteenth century.

Although there were, of course, marriages of love, practical considerations often took priority. In 1835, Chief Justice Edward Jarvis wrote his brother to inform him that "the best thing is undoubtedly for a man to take a wife to look after his domestic establishment." After his wife's death, Jarvis justified remarriage in these words, "such is my social (should I say uxorious) nature that without the fond & endearing affections of a wife to hang upon I should be comparatively miserable." Widowed women usually remarried relatively quickly.

SERVANT PROBLEMS
British traveller and writer Isabella Bird spent six weeks on the Island in the mid-1850s and later recorded her observations about the quality and availability of servants:

> *The difficulty of procuring servants, which is felt from Government House downwards, is one of the great objections of the colony. The few there are know nothing of any individual department of work—for instance, there are neither cooks or housemaids, they are strictly 'helps'—the mistress being expected to take on more than her fair share of the work. They come in and go as they please, and if anything dissatisfies them, they ask for their wages, and depart the same day.... A servant left at an hour's notice, saying "she had never been so insulted before," because her master requested her to put on shoes when she waited at table....*

Father MacEachern's Flock

The early settlers found comfort in the familiar atmosphere of church services. Everyone went to church, except when the snowdrifts became too high for the horses to break through, and most social gatherings revolved around it. At this time, religion played a major role in the community. It determined who could vote, what was learned at school, what types of music were acceptable, and what entertainment could be enjoyed.

Father Angus Bernard MacEachern was one of the most prominent religious figures in early Island history. When he arrived on St. John's Island from Scotland in 1790, the Island had been without a priest for five years. Father MacEachern was responsible for the spiritual welfare of Catholics in St. John's Island and parts of Nova Scotia, Cape Breton, and the Magdalen Islands. For many years, Father MacEachern walked miles through the forests, snowshoed over the winter trails, rode horseback through the fields, and drove a two-wheeled gig over the rough roads to attend to his parish. With little regard for his own safety and health, Father MacEachern embarked on sailing vessels in the summer and on iceboats in the winter. His promotion to bishop in 1821 meant increased responsibilities, with no financial compensation.

Since MacEachern's parishioners included Acadians, Highland Scots, and Irish settlers, it was fortunate that he spoke French, Gaelic, and English. He was admired for his intelligence, sense of humour, and lack of pretension. To fellow Catholics, he was priest and doctor, teacher and friend. As the bishop, MacEachern was largely responsible for the growth in the number of Catholic churches on the Island, from the two that existed when he arrived to fifteen in 1835. He also initiated what would later become St. Dunstan's College. According to historian Edward MacDonald, MacEachern probably hoped that this college would demonstrate Catholic abilities and thus lead the way to Catholics being given the vote. The same personality that endeared MacEachern to his flock helped to foster good relations with the Protestant civil authorities and smoothed the passage of Catholic emancipation in 1830. Prior to this legislation,

ST. ANDREW'S: ITINERANT CHAPEL

St. Andrew's Chapel, circa 1880

When Father MacEachern arrived on Prince Edward Island in 1790 there were only two Catholic churches, and the bishop of Quebec instructed him to build a new church at St. Andrew's. Under Father MacEachern's direction, Scottish settlers constructed St. Andrew's Chapel in 1805. In 1862, the chapel was replaced by a larger church and it lay vacant for two years until 1864, when five hundred men and fifty teams of horses pulled it on runners across twenty-eight kilometres of ice along the Hillsborough River to Charlottetown. Along the way, the chapel fell through thin ice and had to be dragged from the water.

The rescued church was renovated and given to the Sisters of Notre Dame, who converted it into a convent school. The sisters operated the school for more than a hundred years. In 1998, the chapel was divided into four pieces and returned to St. Andrew's. During the subsequent restoration, the original round-headed windows were discovered. Today, the chapel stands as a good example of the eighteenth-century Georgian architecture used by the first settlers from England and Scotland.

Roman Catholics were legally prohibited from voting, holding public office, being lawyers, possessing arms, and owning a horse valued at more than five pounds.

Bishop MacEachern died from a stroke in 1835. He is remembered as the father of Roman Catholicism in Prince Edward Island.

The Wrong Beverage

Alcoholism was rampant on the Island in the early nineteenth century, which was a cause of distress for many Islanders. For example, in 1832, John Lewellin, who had emigrated to the Island eight years earlier, wrote, "rum drinking is the crying sin of North America; and many an otherwise fine fellow does it lead to idleness, to debt to uselessness. Guard against it; abhor the intemperate use of ardent spirits as your deadliest and subtlest foe, that is ready to destroy your faculties, your health, your judgment, your soul!" Drinking to excess was acceptable and even the most respectable people often became so inebriated that they needed to be carried home.

Since milk was scarce and prone to souring, tea and coffee were costly luxuries, and water was sometimes polluted, liquor was kept on the table for daily meals during much of the pioneer period. Mothers gave alcohol to their children on cold mornings to ward off chills, and doctors prescribed alcoholic drinks to cure all kinds of diseases. Although liquor was generally consumed in small quantities at mealtime or for medicinal uses, celebratory imbibing was a different matter. Charlotte Town was home to more than forty taverns, and between 1855 and 1861, the fees from licensing these taverns were its second largest source of income. In 1848, Islanders consumed an average of 2.3 gallons of hard liquor for every man, woman, and child. Rum was the preferred drink.

Entertainment

The range of entertainment on the Island was limited, but almost everyone enjoyed skating, picnics, and horseback riding. Hunting and fishing provided Islanders with both enjoyment and fresh meat. Books and poetry were read aloud at home. Cribbage, whist, backgammon, and chess were popular pastimes, as was smoking clay pipes, chewing tobacco, cigars, or pinches of snuff. Rug hooking and quilting combined enjoyment with practical results, as did picnics and tea parties, which the Islanders held to raise money for worthy projects. Illiteracy and poverty put newspapers beyond the reach of most rural Islanders, although in some cases newspapers were passed from person to person or read aloud.

Early music-making consisted mostly of singing or fiddling, since there were usually very few instruments. Some religious denominations considered the fiddle a tool of the devil, and the only music they approved of was the church choir. It wasn't long, however, before the settlers were singing and dancing to the music of the bagpipes, fiddle, mouth organ, accordion, and mouth harp, although some Protestant churches forbade dancing, as well as cards and the theatre. While the urban upper classes in Charlotte Town waltzed and performed fancy minuets, most Islanders preferred square dances and Scottish and Irish reels.

Every week or so, Island families travelled to the nearest village to sell their produce at the marketplace and buy whatever goods they needed. The Charlotte Town market was the focal point of the town on Wednesdays and Saturdays; there was pandemonium everywhere as customers haggled over prices and children played games in and around the stalls. Carts, horses, and other animals added to the congestion of the market scene.

The predominantly rural population had little leisure time to devote to athletics, especially in the summers. What sports they did play were loosely organized, irregular, and differed from community to community. Only

THE SOCIAL LIVES OF THE WELL-TO-DO

The social life of Dr. John Mackieson's wife typified the leisure activities of the upper classes in Charlottetown. In addition to raising four children, Matilda Mackieson arranged parties and picnics with the other families. Additional entertainment included an amateur theatre, a subscription library, fishing, and winter excursions in open carrioles set on runners to glide over the ice. Matilda also helped raise funds for charity through her membership in the Ladies' Diocesan Church Association, the Charlottetown Ladies' Bible Association, and the Ladies' Benevolent Society.

the wealthier Islanders had time to practise athletics, and team games were possible only in larger communities. Pioneer sports reflected the harsh realities of life: bare-knuckle boxing and wrestling were popular, and gambling was common among all classes.

For a short period, plays were performed in a two-hundred-seat theatre in Charlotte Town. Performances commenced late at night because the actors came to the theatre already dressed and did not want anyone to see their costumes until the play began. There were usually several long delays in the show to allow the performers time to change their costumes in a house across the street.

Robert Harris's depiction of the pillory

Public punishment offered another form of entertainment. Until 1830, Charlotte Town's small jail was primarily a short-term holding cell used only until prisoners could be brought to trial. Punishment was swift. The guilty were put in the stocks or the pillory, branded on the hand with an iron, paraded about town and whipped, or publicly hanged by the neck. Gallows Hill in Charlotte Town always attracted a large crowd. Between 1792 and 1941, eleven individuals were hanged on the Island. The last public execution on the Island took place in 1869.

Education

Because the settlers needed all the help they could get, they often kept their children at home rather than sending them to school. Boys worked in the fields, while girls cooked, mended clothes, made preserves, gardened, and took care of younger children. In 1839, the government tried unsuccessfully to solve the problem of school absenteeism by arranging school vacations during planting and harvesting time in May and October. Thirteen years later, vacations were changed to

School at Canoe Cove *by Robert Harris, circa 1880*

one week in June, one week in October, and the period from December 24 to January 6.

Island teachers were chosen more for their ability to keep order than for their teaching ability. The only qualification to become a teacher was a letter from a clergyman attesting to the teacher's moral character. Although there were already some schools in existence beforehand, it was not until 1825 that the Island legislature sought to promote education by offering to pay some of the costs of school construction and one-sixth of each teacher's salary for schools with at least ten male students over the age of seven. Because most of the teachers' salaries came from fees, poor families could not afford to educate their children and illiteracy remained prevalent.

Island teachers' salaries were so low that some teachers were forced to board with their students' families. In 1837, the official school visitor for the Island, John McNeill, noted this practice with disapproval, writing:

> *I must also mention another practice which is too prevalent in the country, and which, I conceive, is exceedingly injurious to the respectability of the teacher in the eyes of his pupils and consequently, hurtful to his usefulness,—that is receiving his board by going about from house to house; in which case he is regarded both by parents and children, as little better than a common menial.*

Education was neither compulsory nor free. Until 1830, there was virtually no government control over teacher training, textbooks, or curriculum. Still, as the Island became more settled, educational facilities grew faster than the growth of population—between 1837 and 1847, the number of schools increased from 51 to 120, and the number of students grew from about 1,500 to more than 5,000. Most schools were small one-room buildings that were heated by a wood stove. If the school ran out of logs, classes were cancelled for the day. The students, who ranged in age from six to twenty, sat on rough wooden benches that splintered easily. Sometimes forty or fifty children were crowded into one room. Students used outdoor privies, drank from a common pail of water, wrote on slate boards, and made their own rulers, ink, and goose-quill pens. Since blotting paper was unknown at this time, students sprinkled sand over their papers to help the ink dry.

The curriculum at Island schools consisted of little more than the three R's for boys. Girls learned the various domestic skills considered important for their roles as future wives and mothers, such as sewing and knitting. Near the end of the pioneer period, the daughters of the middle and upper classes received instruction in languages (to improve their conversational skills), dancing and music (to entertain guests), and "ornamental subjects" such as needlework. Discipline at Island schools was harsh, as early-nineteenth-century teachers relied for the most part upon memorization and recitation, enforced by corporal punishment.

Life and Death

Disease, accidents, and death were common occurrences in early Prince Edward Island. Since pioneer diets lacked vitamin D, many people suffered from rickets, which led to bowlegs and knock-knees. Wealthier people often ate too much rich food, which caused gout, a painful swelling of the joints in the hands and feet.

Most patients paid their medical bills in farm produce—oatmeal, tea, salt, barley, potatoes, herring, butter, and leather. However, many people preferred to rely on home remedies and patent medicines or to call on a trusted neighbour than to incur the high costs of a doctor's visit.

Early-nineteenth-century medical knowledge had little chance of success. Physicians knew nothing about anaesthetics, bacteria, or sterilization. Surgery often had fatal results and was usually limited to setting fractures, lancing boils, operating on strangulated hernias, and performing amputations. Since physicians had few diagnostic tools, it was natural that they emphasized the significance of such external signs of sickness as unusual perspiration, pulse, urination, skin eruptions, and defecation. These were phenomena that doctors and patients could see, evaluate, and scrutinize for clues of what was wrong. It is not surprising, then, that doctors' most potent weapon was their ability to regulate secretions by bloodletting and purgatives. Raising a blister on one area of the body,

LEECHES HELPED DRAW BLOOD

Early Island physicians employed leeches to treat a wide variety of illnesses. Doctors cleaned the infected part of the body and placed a leech on it to draw the "bad blood" from the patient. Sometimes the leech was held in place by a wine glass. If the leech was slow in taking hold, the doctor might prick his own finger and put a drop of blood on the patient. Once it took hold, the leech continued to draw blood until it was satiated, at which point it fell off the patient. An average leech consumed about a teaspoon of blood. If the bleeding was still insufficient, the doctor applied a poultice to encourage further blood loss. Because they tended to be migratory, leeches had to be carefully counted to ensure that they had not disappeared down a body orifice. In such cases, salt water was administered, followed by either an emetic or an enema, depending upon where the leech had vanished.

practitioners believed, attracted the "morbid excitement" from the affected area to the blistered site, thus reducing the disease's severity.

The physician's art centred on his ability to employ appropriate drugs and techniques to produce a particular physiological effect: opium calmed the patient; quinine, arsenic, and strychnine compounds quickened weak heart rates; mercury produced diarrhea and salivation; laudanum (a tincture of opium) lowered the body's temperature; bloodletting reduced fevers and rapid pulse rates, and removed the "bad blood" from the body; alcohol raised low spirits and weak heart rates; powerful laxatives and emetics cleansed the stomach and bowels. Once they had cleansed their patients' systems, doctors employed tonics or stimulants to restore their systems. For example, when Dr. Mackieson contracted typhus fever, he took wine and other stimulants, and another doctor blistered the back of his neck and applied mustard poultices to the bottom of his feet to draw away the "bad blood." Later, he ate chicken and mutton soups with brown toast to restore his system.

LIFE EXPECTANCY

Life expectancies on the Island in the early nineteenth century tended to be much lower than those of today, partially due to the Islanders' poor diets and hygiene, rustic living conditions, and lack of medical knowledge. Those Islanders that lived relatively long lives often saw their loved ones pass away prematurely. Chief Justice Edward Jarvis, for example, survived two wives and five children. His first wife bore him eight children, three of whom died in infancy and one in childhood. His second wife, Elizabeth, bore him three children, one of whom died shortly after delivery and another who died along with Elizabeth during the birth.

Similarly, Dr. John Mackieson's life was not without its sadness. His youngest son, Augustus, died at the age of twenty-eight after a long illness. A son-in-law also passed away in the prime of his life. A grandson lived only eight months, a granddaughter died at seven months, and another granddaughter lived only three years. Mackieson himself lived into his ninety-fifth year.

Giving Birth

By the middle of the nineteenth century, the average Island woman gave birth to approximately seven children. Although rickets, poor nutrition, and unsanitary conditions resulted in a high infant mortality rate, most births were successful. One of the first choices a woman

DEATH BY FORCEPS

On January 20, 1856, John Tetsen summoned Dr. Mackieson to attend to his pregnant wife. She was twenty years old, and this was to be her first child. Upon his arrival, the physician immediately assumed control from the midwife. Since Mrs. Tetsen had been in labour more than eighteen hours, Dr. Mackieson gave her two doses of ergot to promote abdominal contractions. The drug caused severe discomfort, but succeeded in inducing full labour pains. Unfortunately, the child's head became caught on the pubic bone and Mackieson could not dislodge the baby. Fearing for the mother's health if labour continued much longer, the physician pulled his unsterilized forceps from his bag and inserted them around the baby's head. Since the child was firmly lodged against the pubic bone, Dr. Mackieson had to pull with all his strength. After a little over two hours of medical attendance, the mother delivered a baby boy. Sadly, the child died within the week. Mackieson listed the reason for this death in his medical log as "cause unknown."

had to make after conceiving was who would deliver her child. In most isolated areas of the Island there weren't any doctors, so pregnant women naturally turned to their mothers, aunts, sisters, female friends, or local midwives for help. Sometimes the decision not to summon a doctor was simply a matter of finances, since doctors' fees were too high for many families to afford.

As the century progressed, however, physicians gradually replaced midwives. Some historians argue that the medical profession considered midwives an economic threat and sought to eliminate them through legislation, citing the fact that Island doctors unsuccessfully petitioned the government in 1808 and 1843 to prevent individuals without a licence from practising "Physic, Surgery and Midwifery." Other historians point to the increasing prestige of science and the doctors' skills and anatomical knowledge as reasons for the decline of midwives. As late as 1932, however, the Prince Edward Island Medical Association complained that many women were still using midwives.

Urban Life

Samuel Holland gave Charlotte Town its name in honour of Queen Charlotte, wife of George III of England, and selected it as the capital of the Island, "it being one of the best and central parts of the island, and having the advantage of an immediate and easy communication with the interior parts by means of the three fine rivers of Hillsborough, York, and Elliot." A small stream provided the city with pure drinking

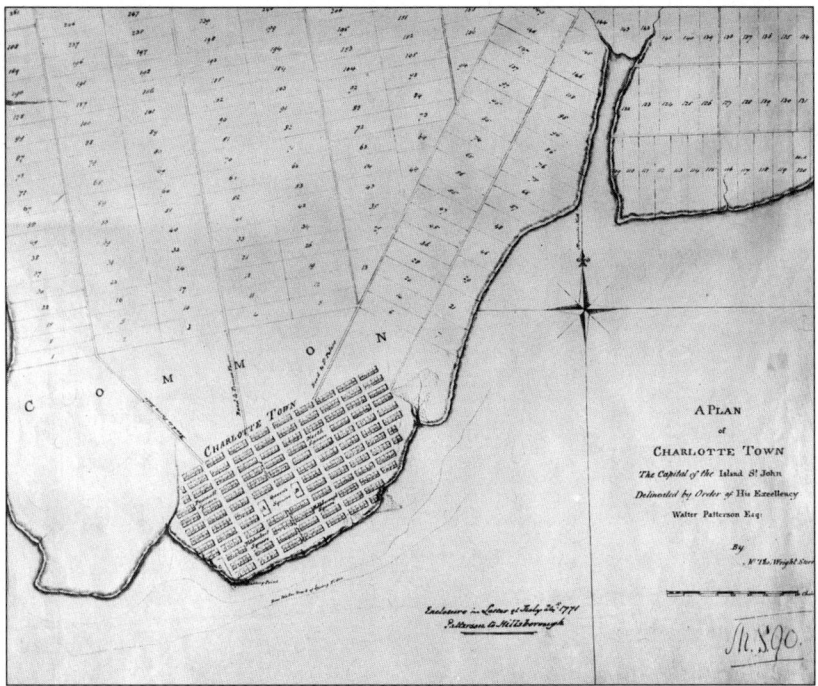

Thomas Wright's original plan for Charlotte Town. The five hundred lots and four green squares in the plan are still recognizable in the town today.

water and Fort Amherst controlled the entrance to the harbour. In addition, Charlotte Town was close to the mainland and was thus well suited for trading with Nova Scotia and Quebec.

In keeping with contemporary town planning notions that structure, harmony, and order should be imposed on nature, surveyors Charles Morris and Thomas Wright created a town plan for Charlotte Town similar to those of London, Bath, and Edinburgh. The streets were laid out in a grid pattern, with a main central area (Queen Square) reserved for important government buildings. Smaller open green spaces were situated in each of the four quadrants of the grid. Beyond the five hundred town lots (each of which measured 84 feet by 160 feet) lay a belt of farmland (The Royalty) where urban dwellers could grow their own food. Streets leaving the waterfront were one hundred feet wide to guard against fire. The wide, dimly lit streets often turned into mud holes in the spring and fall and into

Charlottetown, Prince Edward Island in 1843 *by Fanny Bayfield. Charlotte Town's first market, the round house—pictured here, centre—was built in 1823.*

dust bowls in the summer.

Charlotte Town grew slowly. The first Island governor, Walter Patterson, was probably quite shocked when he stepped ashore in Charlotte Town in 1770. Even though it was the capital of the Island, there were only two "decent" buildings in the entire town. Between 1798 and 1821, Charlotte Town's population increased from 416 to approximately 2,000 people, who inhabited three hundred drab wooden buildings. By the mid-nineteenth century, most Charlotte Town residents lived in houses that stood back from the main roads and had small windows, since large plates of glass were expensive to import. The city had two fire engines, which required sixteen people to pump the handles, and a bucket brigade to supply the firefighters with water. To prevent fire damage, homeowners were required to keep a ladder and two leather buckets of water, and to sweep their chimneys regularly.

The growth of Charlottetown (as it was spelled after 1855) to sixty-five hundred inhabitants in 1855 presented serious sanitation and health problems. Lacking scavenger services, the citizens of Charlottetown dumped their refuse in the streets. Excrement from

Queen Street, Charlottetown, circa 1860s

outdoor privies soaked through the ground, contaminating the shallow wells that provided the city with drinking water. Pigs rooted through the garbage in the streets or in the offal piles generated by the city's slaughterhouses and tanneries. In 1848, a census taker for the city noted:

> *In procuring the material for the preceding statistics Nuisances came under my nose that were of an extremely repulsive character and must inevitable engender and propagate Disease. I have seen many families in extreme destitution of the means of subsistence, living in places resembling Pig Styes more than the dwellings of human beings; the squalid misery of many living in the back streets, lanes, and alleys, and the inferiority of the air they inhale, must prove very injurious to the health of the community in general.*

Despite the worsening sanitation situation, the city did not appoint a permanent health officer until 1877.

DIRTY PEOPLE

Keeping clean in nineteenth-century Prince Edward Island was hard work—there was no running water, bath water had to be carried from outside and heated over the fire, and clothes had to be washed and wrung out by hand and hung out to dry. Since there were no toothbrushes, people used pieces of cloth and salt to clean their teeth. Many people chewed tobacco and spit the juice on the ground.

Fashionable Urban Wear

Fashionable Charlotte Town women wore whalebone corsets to keep their silhouettes straight and slim. By the 1840s, women's bodices were heavily boned and very stiff, their sleeves were becoming more elaborate, and their dress waists began to drop. Because of the drab, dull surroundings, women wore bright colours whenever possible.

Women of the elite followed a complex set of rules regarding appropriate dress. Young ladies emphasized their youth and innocence by wearing simple, pastel-coloured dresses. Such modesty, they believed, would be attractive to potential husbands. Older women wore heavier fabrics and rich dark colours to emphasize their wisdom and authority.

Upper-class urban men were clean-shaven, with their sideburns reaching to the bottom of their earlobes. Their hair was usually curled over their foreheads. Top hats made of beaver or wool were popular. Men used suspenders to hold up their trousers, which buttoned from knee to ankle. The fly was invented in 1825 and was in common use by 1840.

Chapter Seven
Island Politics and the Land Problem

In 1763, Britain placed St. John's Island and Cape Breton under the Nova Scotian authorities in Halifax. Six years later, after intense lobbying by Island landlords, the Island became a separate colony on the condition that the landowners pay for the salaries of the civil service. On July 14, 1769, Walter Patterson was appointed "Governor-in-Chief" of the Island. Patterson had fought in North America during the Seven Years' War and in 1767 he and his brother had received Lot 19 in the land lottery. The following year, Patterson was one of the landowners who worked to get the Island separated from Nova Scotia.

The new governor faced a daunting task. The colony was almost a total wilderness. Few people on the Island had administrative experience, and the colony's future development rested on the governor's ability to collect quit rent from the landlords. The population numbered little more than three hundred people, most of whom were Acadians who did not speak English and whose loyalty was suspect. Charlotte Town had only two decent buildings and a few log huts. There was no place of worship, no courthouse, and no jail. Complaining about the lack of a jail, in October 1770 Patterson wrote, "there is not one House, or place in or near this Town, that would confine a Man one Hour contrary to his inclination."

Initially, Patterson was kept busy attending to his everyday needs and building a house for himself. He was expecting more officials to join him on the Island that first year, but the conditions were so bad that he warned them not to come until later. "There is not a house to put your head into," he lamented, "and if you do not bring food and other goods to last until June, you will starve because there is not a loaf of bread, or the flour to make a loaf, to be bought on the Island."

ISLAND POLITICS, 1763-1854

1763: The Island is annexed to Nova Scotia
1764-5: Samuel Holland completes his survey
1767: The land lottery takes place
1769: The Island is given its own governor and civil administration
1773: The first House of Assembly convenes
1799: St. John's Island is renamed Prince Edward Island
1830: Island Roman Catholics receive full civil rights
1851: Responsible government is granted
1854: The Reciprocity Treaty with the United States is signed

Walter Patterson

Walter Patterson and Early Island Government

Walter Patterson's most important task as governor was to establish a government. In September 1770, he appointed an executive council of seven men to make laws for the colony. The British government had instructed him to choose twelve men, but Patterson replied that he could find no more than seven qualified people. The council's responsibility was to advise and assist the governor in overseeing the Island. Unfortunately, most of the councillors had been trained as soldiers and knew very little about government.

Since the British Colonial Office doubted that there were sufficient numbers of respectable citizens to form a separate legislative council, the executive council served as the legislative branch of the Island's legislature until 1839. As the Island's population grew, the British government decided to give Island males a voice in their own government by creating an elected assembly. Such a body, the British minister in charge of the colonies

Province House in Queen Square, Charlottetown, circa 1860. Completed in 1847, this neo-classical stone building was designed and built by local architect Isaac Smith to accommodate the Provincial Legislature. It represented the epitome of Island craftsmanship and optimism. It still houses the Provincial Legislature.

stated, "would be the foundation of [the Island's] future welfare and prosperity." Patterson allowed all male Protestants who were twenty-one years of age or older to vote. The first election was held in Charlotte Town on July 4, 1773. Eighteen men were elected to the assembly to help the governor and his council pass laws. Patterson decided on eighteen members because he wished "to have those who were about to be chosen, as respectable as possible," and he didn't think there were many more men who "would make a very tolerable appearance." Lacking a suitable location, the legislature initially met at the Crossed Keys Tavern in Charlotte Town. Only Nova Scotia has an older legislature in Canada.

The most pressing problem on the Island in the early 1770s was the landlords' continuing refusal to pay their quit rents. This money was needed to pay the governor's salary, erect public buildings, build roads, and help run the government. By 1775, the landlords had paid less than £3,000 of the £6,000 then due, and the Island's civil servants were left in a precarious situation. The lack of funds was partly solved in 1777, when Governor Patterson convinced the British government to pay the costs of governing the Island.

Although the legislative assembly did not become particularly powerful until the achievement of responsible government in the 1850s, it provided Island residents with a chance to inform the governor of their opinions and needs. The governor, however, was not required to carry out the assembly's wishes. As well, because St. John's Island was a British colony, no bill could become law until it was approved by the British government. British imperial interests thus took precedence over local Island needs.

Elections: Rum and Riots

Until 1787, Islanders had to travel to Charlotte Town to vote. Polls stayed open for several days to allow distant settlers time to vote and to enable people to vote in every constituency in which they held property. Elections were often wild affairs. Islanders voted by raising their hands or by yelling out the name of the candidates they favoured. Since voting was not a secret, it was easy to bribe the voters, and candidates sometimes offered free liquor to everyone who promised to vote for them.

Each candidate's supporters took turns parading to the polling area, singing and waving banners. These displays of support sometimes degenerated into brawls between different ethnic or religious groups. The most infamous election brawl on the Island took place in 1847 near Belfast, an area that consisted of Loyalists, Scottish Protestants, and Irish Roman Catholics. Election violence the previous year had

---

EARLY LAWS

During its first few years, the Island government passed hundreds of laws on all sorts of topics. Several of these early ordinances illustrate the nature of the colony at this time:

- Ship captains were prevented from carrying away settlers who were in debt.
- A reward of fifteen shillings was offered to anyone who killed a bear and had its snout as proof.
- In an attempt to reduce the animals who preyed on Island livestock, five shillings were offered for the snout of a lynx.

VOTING DAY

A pencil-and-ink drawing of voting day by Robert Harris

In 1867, local historian Henry Mellick described election days at the time in the *Summerside Progress*: "Without plenty of rum a candidate's chances for success were very poor, however good he or his party or platform might be.... One time the barrel supplied by a candidate was all drunk early in the day. The candidate was at another polling place several miles away. A messenger was sent with all possible haste to have him send another barrel of rum. The situation was desperate; he was informed that unless he sent another barrel at once he would not get another vote. The rum was sent immediately and the voters poured in like a river and carried the candidate to a glorious victory."

caused many people to question the results, and the government had called a by-election for March 1. Ethnic, religious, and class tensions remained high. In two separate incidents during the election, mobs of Irish and Scottish tenants attacked one other with clubs, fists, and feet. When the electoral officials attempted to assist the victims, they were also beaten. At least three people were killed, and the blood of countless others stained the freshly fallen snow.

The Great Land Swindle

In 1781, Walter Patterson decided to auction eleven townships belonging to landlords who had not paid their quit rents. The governor kept the date of the auction secret and thus the only buyers were Patterson and his friends. No money changed hands in the transactions, since the buyers claimed the land in lieu of the salaries they were owed for their official government duties. The governor obtained three whole and four half townships for himself, plus an additional seventy thousand acres in the names of four English acquaintances.

Patterson's actions created a storm. The Island landlords complained to the British government that they had not been informed of the sale and pointed out that the governor and his friends had taken the best land on the Island, mostly from individuals whom Patterson disliked. The powerful Stewart and DesBrisay families were particularly angered by the auction, which left them with only a few lots. Their dislike of the governor grew to hatred when it was revealed that he had "stolen the heart" of Peter Stewart's wife while her husband was sick in bed with rheumatism. In retaliation, the Stewarts and DesBrisays petitioned the British government to remove Governor Patterson.

Although Patterson was ordered to return to England in 1786 "as soon as may be" to answer the charges against him, he refused to comply for another three years. When Patterson finally arrived in Great Britain, he was bankrupt. His enemies had assumed control of his property on St. John's Island and had sold it for much less than it was worth. Walter Patterson died in London in 1798 in poverty and disgrace. As one landowner said of him, Patterson was a man of "an amazing cleverness...mixed with an equal proportion of folly and madness," who "rose from nothing, & would have done extremely well, had he known where to stop...."

The Land Question

In 1819, absentee British landlord James Townshend hired Edward Abell, an Island farmer and merchant, to manage Lot 56 and collect rent from his ninety tenants. Abell was known for being rather

ANOTHER NAME CHANGE

In 1780, the Island government noted that since there were at least eight ports, rivers, and forts named St. John in the Atlantic colonies, mail was frequently sent to the wrong place, and they renamed the Island "New Ireland" in honour of Governor Patterson's homeland. The British government, however, refused to accept the name, arguing that "New Ireland" had already been taken by another colony. "You may," the British minister in charge of the colonies replied, "change the name to New Guernsey or New Anglesea." These two suggestions were rejected by the Island government.

Finally, in 1799, the Island government named the colony Prince Edward Island, in honour of the son of King George III. Prince Edward had never visited the colony, but he had ordered that its defences be improved. Ironically, unbeknownst to the Island government, the prince had also suggested that St. John's Island be rejoined with Nova Scotia, an idea that was anathema to them. If the government officials had known this fact, the province would probably not have its present name.

His Royal Highness, Prince Edward

hard-headed, and he frequently applied for foreclosures against tenants who did not pay their rent. Patrick Pearce, an Irish tenant in Lot 56, owned a beautiful black horse that both Abell and his wife coveted for its beauty and the social status that it would bring them, and Abell approached Pearce with an offer to buy the horse. When Pearce refused to sell the horse, Abell demanded that he pay his rent immediately. Pearce paid his rent, but among the payment were several Spanish coins that were good on the Island but were not legal tender in Great Britain. Abell refused to accept these coins and threatened to take Pearce's horse.

As there were no banks on the Island, Pearce went to his neighbours for help. They traded their British coins for his Spanish coins, and Pearce hurried back to his farm. However, when he arrived, Edward Abell and his servant were leading his horse away. Abell refused to accept the new coins and demanded even more money. Pearce was furious, but he set off to borrow the money from his friends.

When Pearce returned, Abell again refused to accept the payment and the two argued angrily. Pearce grabbed his musket, which had a long bayonet, from the cabin and stabbed Abell twice before the servant could stop him. When the servant went for help, Pearce escaped into the woods.

Abell died four days later and the government offered a large reward for Pearce's capture. Although the reward would have paid the average tenant's rent for four years, his neighbours protected him. Dressed in women's clothes, Pearce escaped by boat to the mainland. He was never found, and for a long time his house remained abandoned, as many people believed it was haunted.

This sensational tale illustrates the land problems that bedevilled Prince Edward Island for over a century and distinguished Island politics from the political situation in the other British North American colonies. Initially, most Island landlords considered their lands investment properties, speculative ventures in an unknown region. Few of them took sufficient interest to promote settlement or even to visit the Island. As a result, by 1797 only twenty-six of the sixty-seven lots had been settled in accordance with the terms of the original grant. In twenty-three of the townships there were no settlers at all. A few years later, a visiting British soldier concluded that the "Principal Cause of the backwardness of the Colony" was "impolitic grants of large tracts of land."

Over time, some wealthy Islanders acquired large tracts of land that they rented out to local settlers. The absentee landowners hired local agents to manage their property and collect rent from the tenants. By the early 1830s, landlords controlled about ninety percent of the colony's farmland, and two-thirds of the rural population consisted of tenants or squatters. Since it took many years of backbreaking work to build a farm that generated sufficient income to pay the rent, most tenants soon fell behind in their rent payments. Nonpayment could lead to eviction, without compensation for improvements. Consequently, relations between landlords and tenants tended to be less than amiable.

During the first thirty years of the nineteenth century, several unsuccessful attempts were made to solve the land problem. Since the tenants believed that the British government's failure to help them was due to a lack of information, most of their efforts were confined to such legitimate actions as petitions and memorials. However, the landlords who lived on the Island were often members of the government and were thereby able to prevent the Island government from doing anything that might harm their interests, and the absentee landlords in Great Britain were wealthy and powerful enough to convince the British government not to interfere.

William Cooper: The People's Champion

William Cooper's decision to enter politics in 1830 brought the land question into the limelight. Cooper was born in England, and after spending many years at sea, in 1819 he settled near Bay Fortune, where Edward Abell had been murdered. Cooper succeeded Abell as Lord James Townshend's agent and initiated several profitable projects, including arranging for the construction of a gristmill on the property. He also helped the tenant farmers find markets for their produce and convinced Townshend to allow the tenants to pay their rent with manual labour or agricultural products.

Lord Townshend dismissed Cooper from his position in 1829, although the reasons he did so remain unclear. Cooper's political enemies later claimed that he had stolen funds. Whatever the reason, after this incident Cooper underwent a change of heart amounting almost to a religious conversion and became a bitter enemy of the Island landlords.

Cooper ran for political office in 1831, and since he had always sought to help the tenants, Bay Fortune gave him its support and he was elected to the assembly. Cooper believed that the best way to

William Cooper

solve the land question and provide justice for the tenants was to establish a special court known as an escheat court. Escheat, pronounced *iss chéet*, is the process by which unimproved lands revert to the Crown and become subject to reallocation. The escheat court would research which landlords had not paid their quit rents to the government or settled the required number of people on their land. The government would then confiscate the land of those landlords who had not lived up to their agreements, and sell or give this land to the tenants. The idea of an escheat court had originated on the Island in 1797, but Cooper's actions gave it momentum.

Cooper organized tenant meetings throughout the Island, encouraged the tenants not to pay their rents, and formed the Escheat Party. The escheat movement created an Island-wide network of community groups that organized meetings and rallies, circulated petitions, and debated political strategy. Thousands of people participated in all sorts of public demonstrations, and women were as militant as men. For example, when Constable Donald McVarish was confronted by an angry group of three male and two female tenants, he drew his pistol and pointed it at Isabella MacDonald, who, although well-advanced in pregnancy, appeared to be the most violent member of the group. The tenants stripped McVarish of his gun and forced him to leave and promise never to return, after which Isabella MacDonald gave him a parting slap with a board.

Angry groups of tenants threatened rent collectors with pitchforks, stones, and other crude weapons. A few rent collectors were hit with frozen cow dung or had the tails of their prize horses cut off. Although some tenants were able to avoid paying rent, many were arrested or evicted from their land. At a meeting of seven hundred angry tenants at Hay River in 1836, Cooper's inflammatory words and actions so annoyed Sir Charles FitzRoy, the lieutenant-governor of the Island, that he ordered Cooper to apologize. When Cooper refused, the governor banned him from the assembly. The people, however, showed that they supported Cooper's ideas, as the Escheat Party won eighteen of the twenty-four seats in the ensuing election and Cooper returned to the assembly.

Lieutenant-Governor Sir Charles Augustus FitzRoy

In 1838, the assembly sent Cooper to London to convince the British government of the need for an escheat court. To save money, Cooper travelled third-class aboard a lumber ship. FitzRoy gave Cooper a letter of introduction to the corridors of power, but he also wrote a secret letter to London in which he criticized Cooper's character and attempted to discredit his cause. Cooper, he wrote, was an "extremely artful person and possessed of much low cunning." Those few individuals who supported him, the letter continued, were "extremely ignorant and illiterate farmers of the poorer class" who were "duped and led away by Cooper."

Cooper spent two months in England trying to convince the Colonial Office of the justness of his cause. Although he provided a variety of documents and petitions, one of which had three thousand signatures, he was unsuccessful. A court of escheat, the Colonial Office declared, would "unsettle the minds of the inhabitants" and "shake the rights of property."

Later that year, the Escheat Party won another landslide victory, and the assembly sent Cooper back to England in 1839 to argue its case. Once again, however, Lieutenant-Governor FitzRoy undermined Cooper's mission. For three months the British government put Cooper off with delays and excuses. He finally returned to the Island a defeated man. Great Britain, it seemed, would never accept the idea of an escheat court.

Back on the Island, Cooper was criticized for not pursuing the tenants' cause with more vigour, and although he was elected again in 1842, the escheat cause lost its momentum. Meanwhile, the landlords used the local courts to crush rural resistance and effectively end the escheat movement. Justice Jarvis, for example, sentenced one man to a jail term of six months and another to four months for rent resistance, despite the fact that the offence of one of the men was simply being among a crowd that peacefully opposed the rent collector.

In 1849, Cooper and his family sailed to California during the gold rush. Cooper returned to the Island shortly thereafter, but his family remained in California. Although Cooper remained in the Island legislature until 1862, he gradually lost interest in politics and turned to shipbuilding. He died in 1867.

The Struggle for Responsible Government

George Coles continued the opposition to the landlords that Cooper had started. He was more moderate than Cooper; instead of using violence and threats to get his way, Coles believed that Great Britain would accept changes only if they occurred slowly and gradually.

Coles was born on a farm in Charlottetown Royalty. After helping his father on the farm for many years, he started his own business and soon became the largest producer of liquor in the colony. He later acquired a steam mill, imported carding machines, and rented houses in Charlottetown. In addition, Coles managed a farm, which the *Islander* described as "one of the best managed and most productive in the Island."

Coles was elected to the assembly in 1842. He was a controversial politician whose intemperate language resulted in several attempts to ban him from the assembly. British traveller and writer Isabella Bird described Coles as "a self-made and self-educated man," who, "by his own energy, industry and perseverance" raised himself to political power, and argued, "if his manners have not all the finish of polite society, and if he does sometimes say 'Me and governor,' his energy is not less to be admired." B. W. A. Sleigh, however, wrote scathingly of Coles, reporting, "the highest Member of the Executive Council keeps a grog-shop."

Coles believed that the first step toward solving the land problem was to change the Island's form of government. At that time, the Island government was largely controlled by the lieutenant-governor, who was appointed by the British government. The lieutenant-governor listened to the advice of the executive council

George Coles

(which he appointed) and to the assembly (which was elected), but he did not have to accept their advice. The executive council was dominated by a small group of related families who controlled much of the Island's wealth. All bills passed by the assembly required the executive council's approval before being sent to the lieutenant-governor. Since the lieutenant-governor and the executive council were often sympathetic to the landlords or were landlords themselves, the assembly's wishes were usually ignored.

Coles believed that the only way the tenants could get a fair deal was to make the assembly more powerful, and that the best way to do this was through responsible government. Under responsible government, the appointed executive council is answerable to the elected assembly and must have its support in order to remain in office. The idea of responsible government was not new. Reformers in Nova Scotia, New Brunswick, and the other British North American colonies were also struggling to achieve it. Although Nova Scotia was granted responsible government in 1848, the British government thought that the people on the Island were too poor and too uneducated to make it work.

Edward Whelan

Edward Whelan supported Coles's political philosophy. Whelan was born in Ireland and immigrated to Nova Scotia in 1831. Possessed of a good education, Whelan assumed the editorship of the semi-weekly *Palladium* in Charlotte Town in 1843. The paper's objective, he stated, was "to investigate and assail, if not remedy, the evils which have grown out of the Landocracy System, a system whose principle is 'monopoly,' whose effect is oppression." Despite these strong words, Whelan charted a conservative course and refused to support escheat until responsible government was achieved.

Through the pages of the *Examiner*, which he started in 1847, Whelan swung the Irish tenants behind Coles's Reform Party. His writing had a caustic wit that both angered and entertained. Several times he appeared in court to answer charges of libel and "riot and assault." Although Whelan was elected to the assembly in 1846 and was described by one politician as a "brilliant, impassioned, exciting" orator, he rarely spoke in the assembly.

In February 1850, Coles and Whelan's Reform Party won eighteen of the twenty-four seats in the assembly and subsequently clashed with the lieutenant-governor over the idea of responsible government. Ultimately, the British government granted the Island responsible government in 1851 because it had already allowed it in Nova Scotia, New Brunswick, and the Canadas. George Coles became the Island's first premier. The Island was now semi-independent—the colonial government was responsible for everything except foreign trade and defence, and the lieutenant-governor retained veto power to protect the landlords' property rights.

The Tenant League

The new government's first attempts to help the tenants failed, as in 1851 the British authorities rejected a proposal for a tax on estates in excess of five hundred acres and a bill that would have forced landlords to reimburse evicted tenants for improvements they had made to the land. The Land Purchase Act of 1853 was more successful. This bill allowed the Island government to buy any estate over one thousand acres from a willing landlord and sell the land to tenants at a maximum of three hundred acres each.

Progress was being made, but change came slowly. Although a few estates were bought and resold, many landlords refused to sell their land, and the Island government had little money with which to buy it. The tenants hoped that the British government would either lend money to the Island government to help them purchase estates or force the landlords to sell their land at a fair price. When the British government rejected these solutions, the tenants decided to take matters into their own hands.

Several public meetings in 1864 resulted in the creation of a Tenant League. Each member of the league pledged to withhold his rent and to support other tenants who refused to honour their leases. By depriving the landlords of this revenue, the league hoped to force them to sell their land at reasonable rates. In less than a year, membership in the league swelled to about eleven thousand people. Politicians were excluded from the league, as they were perceived to have failed the tenants.

After many protests organized by the Tenant League, the Island government finally sent for the British troops in Halifax to help control the situation. The government also vindictively dismissed those teachers and magistrates who openly sympathized with the Tenant League.

Persuaded by the disturbances incited by the Tenant League, some landlords sold their holdings. The large estate that had belonged to shipping magnate Samuel Cunard, for example, was sold in 1866. By 1871, only one-quarter of the Island remained in the hands of the large proprietors.

FLETCHER OUTSMARTS THE SHERIFF

On March 17, 1865, the Tenant League organized a march through Charlottetown and about five hundred demonstrators marched through the city. During this otherwise peaceful demonstration, Deputy Sheriff James Curtis attempted to arrest a tenant named Sam Fletcher for non-payment of his rent. Fletcher knocked the sheriff to the ground and escaped, and the government ordered the sheriff to organize a posse to arrest Fletcher. As the posse marched the thirty kilometres to Fletcher's farm, the tenants along the way blew their trumpets to warn Fletcher of its advance.

It was April and the clay roads had been reduced to mud. This, plus the political divisions within the conscripted posse, did not help the men's spirits. It was Sam Fletcher's tactics, however, that created the most consternation and exposed the posse to public ridicule. No two stories are identical, but all agree that Fletcher outsmarted the sheriff and his men. At a blacksmith's shop near Vernon River, a crude fort manned with cannons delayed the posse until closer inspection revealed that the fort was constructed of old stove pipes and the men who manned the guns were only straw scarecrows with paper faces and nightcaps. Later, as the posse approached Fletcher's property, the men were amazed to see him calmly leaning against his gatepost. After carefully surrounding him, the men were embarrassed once again. The clothes were Fletcher's, but the body was made of straw. Dispirited, the posse returned to Charlottetown without their man.

After the fiasco, Edward Whelan wrote scathingly in the *Examiner*: "Up to Friday last, Sam Fletcher was an insignificant individual. He is now the hero of the hour; and the ease with which he had turned his back upon the concentrated force of the county ... [had] thereby covered it with ridicule." Fletcher was never apprehended, and became a popular symbol of successful resistance to authority.

When the Island entered Confederation in 1873 the federal government provided $800,000 to help solve the land problems. Two years later, the provincial government passed an act to determine the price at which proprietors would be compelled to sell their land to the government. Later that year, the government purchased 187,700 acres of Island land at $1.63 per acre. By 1895, it had bought and resold all of the Island estates and most of the tenants had become property owners.

CHAPTER EIGHT
Confederation

The 1860s were important years in world history. The United States experienced a civil war, which resulted in the official end of slavery; purchased Alaska from Russia; and forced Japan to open its borders to Western trade and ideas. Russian serfs gained their freedom from the landowners. Germany and Italy became nations.

For Canadians, 1867 is one of the most important dates in history. This was the year Canada was born. Three years earlier, British North America (BNA) had been a collection of sparsely populated colonies and territories that knew very little about one another. Of the approximately 3.34 million inhabitants of BNA, about three-quarters lived in Central Canada (present-day Ontario and Quebec). The city of Montreal had more inhabitants than Prince Edward Island.

The Lead-Up to Confederation

In 1841, Great Britain reunited Upper and Lower Canada (the future Ontario and Quebec, respectively) into the United Province of Canada. By the 1860s, however, this union was becoming impossible to govern. The English-speaking inhabitants of Upper Canada disliked and distrusted the Roman Catholic French Canadians in the eastern half of the province. The feeling was mutual. Unable to achieve a stable majority, the government floundered in indecision and the economy stagnated. Petty jealousies, personality conflicts, and religious and ethnic differences made it difficult for any one political party to gain a majority of the seats in the provincial assembly. To make matters worse, the United States was engaged in a bloody civil war, and some American politicians were talking about marching north into Canada at war's end to avenge Britain's assistance to the South.

On June 14, 1864, George Brown, a prominent journalist and leading politician from Upper Canada, rose in the assembly and announced

George Brown

John A. Macdonald

that he was ready to accept any solution to solve the political deadlock. "I desire no greater honour for my children," Brown declared, "than that I had a hand, however humble, in bringing about a solution to our difficulties." The members of the assembly stood and cheered. Soon afterwards, Brown joined forces with the colony's most prominent politicians, John A. Macdonald and George-Étienne Cartier, in what became known as the Great Coalition. The three men and their parties worked together to bring about Confederation.

Confederation was not a new idea. Similar schemes had been suggested ever since the American Revolution. The Great Coalition's plan was to separate the United Province of Canada into two provinces, Ontario and Quebec, and add the four Atlantic colonies to create a separate country. Each province would have its own government for local matters. A House of Commons in Ottawa, to which each province would elect members according to the size of its population, would make decisions on matters affecting more than one province. Before the coalition could put its plan into effect, however, it would have to win over the Atlantic colonies and convince their governments to come on board.

Danger from the South

In 1861, a bloody civil war erupted in the United States between the Northern and the Southern states. Later that year, the United States and Great Britain came to the brink of war. For two months, the British North American colonies feared a war in which they would be in the middle. With such a long Canadian-American border, and without a railway to move troops quickly, British North America could be easily conquered.

Confederation, argued its supporters, would not only provide unified leadership in the region, it would also result in the building of a railway between the colonies that would promote inter-regional trade and help defend the country against American aggression. George Brown epitomized the prevalent anti-American attitudes of many Upper Canadians when he stated,

George-Étienne Cartier

> *The Americans are now a warlike people. They have large armies, a powerful navy, an unlimited supply of warlike munitions, and the carnage of war has to them been stripped of its horrors. The American side of our lines already bristles with works of defence, and unless we are willing to live at the mercy of our neighbours, we, too, must put our country in a state of efficient preparation.*

Not everyone agreed with Brown. Wilfrid Laurier, the future prime minister of Canada, declared that attempting to defend against the United States was like being "armed with an egg-shell to stop a bullet."

American decisions also affected the Canadian economy. In 1854, British North America and the United States had signed a Reciprocity Treaty that admitted British North American natural products into the United States without paying duties, and allowed American fishers into British waters. Each colony had benefited and Canadian exports in timber, grain, coal, livestock, and fish had increased.

When the United States announced in 1865 that it intended to terminate the Reciprocity Treaty the following year, many people in BNA began to search for new markets for their goods. Confederation, its supporters argued, would remove the existing trade barriers between colonies and improve intercolonial trade. Central Canadians could ship grain and manufactured products to the Maritimes, and the Maritimes could send coal and fish to Central Canada. A railway would facilitate this trade and provide Central Canadian merchants with a year-round ice-free port on the east coast.

The Charlottetown Conference

The Great Coalition's first task in bringing about Confederation was to persuade the Atlantic colonies that Confederation was a good idea. Fortunately for them, Nova Scotia, New Brunswick, and Prince Edward Island had been debating the possibility of a Maritime union, and the Canadian government asked to be invited to their next meeting.

Some Maritime politicians believed that a Maritime union would turn the three relatively weak Maritime colonies into a single, more powerful body and eliminate such problems as coping with three different currencies and laws. However, each colony was protective of its own rights, and contact among the three provinces, especially in winter, was sporadic.

Although the Island politicians were unenthusiastic about the possibility of a Maritime union, they agreed to attend a conference on the topic—but only if the meeting was held on the Island. When the Canadian politicians learned about the plans for this conference, they asked permission to attend and present their own proposal, which the Maritime governments granted. The Maritime governments then

The Fathers of Confederation in Charlottetown, September 1864. The Island's delegates were Premier John Hamilton Gray, Edward Palmer, William Henry Pope, Andrew Archibald Macdonald, and George Coles.

agreed on a place and date for the meeting: in Charlottetown on September 1, 1864.

Most Islanders displayed a general lack of interest in the conference. When the delegates from Nova Scotia and New Brunswick arrived in Charlottetown, there was no one to meet them. Everyone, it seemed, was at the circus, which was making its first appearance on the Island in twenty-one years. When the Canadians arrived the next day aboard the steamboat *Queen Victoria*, only William Henry Pope, the provincial secretary, was present to greet them. A fisher rowed him out to the *Queen Victoria* in an old oyster boat with two jars of molasses in the stern and a barrel of flour in the bow.

The conference delegates, now known as the Fathers of Confederation, met in Charlottetown's Province House behind closed doors. The Maritime delegation agreed to postpone discussion of a Maritime union until it had heard the Canadian proposal. Over the eight days of the conference, vigorous and reasoned speeches from Macdonald, Cartier, Brown, and others regarding the economic, nationalistic, and

THE TABLE GROANED UNDER THE CHOICEST VIANDS

The Charlottetown *Examiner* described the final supper for the delegates, held in Province House, as "the most brilliant Fête that has ever occurred in Charlottetown," and reported:

> ...from substantial rounds of beef and splendid hams, to the more delicate trifles of the cuisine, were in great abundance—salmon, lobster salad, oysters prepared in every shape and style, all the different kinds of fowl which the season and the market could afford—all vegetable delicacies peculiar to the season—pastry in all forms—fruits in almost every variety—wines of the choicest vintage—were in greatest profusion, leaving scarcely an inch of vacant space on the wide table.

military benefits of Confederation convinced the Maritime representatives that it might be a good idea, and they agreed to meet again in the fall in Quebec City to hammer out a constitution for the new country.

Along with being the precursor to Confederation, the Charlottetown Conference is remembered for its parties, elegant dinners, and excursions about the Island. The Canadians brought thirteen thousand dollars worth of champagne along with them to facilitate the discussions, and the Islanders wined and dined the delegates in style. The crowning event was a grand ball at Province House. From ten at night until one in the morning, the delegates and their wives danced to the sounds of two bands. Dinner was served after midnight, followed by three hours of speeches. The next day, the delegates left for a tour of the Maritimes before proceeding to Quebec City.

The Quebec Conference

Thirty-three delegates, including two from Newfoundland, attended the conference in Quebec City, which was held between October 10 and 27, 1864. The seven delegates from Prince Edward Island were George Coles, John H. Gray, T. H. Haviland, A. A. Macdonald, Edward Palmer, W. H. Pope, and Edward Whelan. It rained the entire seventeen days of the conference, dampening the spirits of those in attendance. One reporter wrote, "It is raining. It rains every day, making the stay in Quebec -- normally so gay and amusing when the weather is fine -- disagreeable in the extreme."

Unlike the festive mood at Charlottetown, arguments raged back and forth at the Quebec Conference. Constitution-making was serious business, and the delegates were vigilant in protecting their colonies' interests. It soon became evident that the Canadians did not envision that the Island would have much to say regarding national matters. Instead of having provincial equality in the Senate (as in the United States, where every state elected two senators), there was to be regional equality; the Atlantic colonies, Ontario, and Quebec were each to receive the same number of senators. The Islanders sought six seats in the House of Commons, but the Canadian delegates insisted on the principle of representation by population, and Prince Edward Island was allotted only five members to represent its population of about eighty thousand people. As well, when the Island delegates requested $800,000 to buy the properties of the landlords and end decades of turmoil, the other delegates rejected the idea.

After seventeen days of heated debate, the delegates drew up a tentative constitution for the new country. They then returned home to convince their governments to accept these suggestions, which were termed the Seventy-Two Resolutions.

Acceptance and Rejection
Upper Canadians were the most enthusiastic supporters of Confederation. It would give them their own province, improve their economy, allow expansion to the west, and provide protection against the United States. As the most populous province, Ontario would have the most members in the House of Commons, giving them a significant amount of power in the decision-making process. Since many French-Canadian politicians had not read the proposed constitution and could not understand English well enough to follow the debates in the assembly, they relied on Cartier and the Roman Catholic clergy to guide them. In 1865, the Canadas voted in favour of Confederation. Now it was up to the Atlantic colonies.

Confederation was more controversial in the Atlantic colonies. Prior to Confederation, there was very little economic and social contact between the Atlantic colonies and Central Canada. Newspapers focused on local and international events rather than on the adjoining colonies. In terms of economic relations, only 2.1 percent of Prince

Edward Island's imports and 0.6 percent of its exports involved Central Canada. Based on population, the Atlantic colonies would have only forty-six out of the two hundred seats in the House of Commons and thus could be outvoted by Central Canada.

Because of New Brunswick's geographic position between Nova Scotia and Quebec, a union between the Maritime colonies and the Province of Canada was not possible without its consent. Premier Leonard Tilley's pro-Confederation New Brunswick government, however, was already unpopular. In addition, many New Brunswick merchants and bankers feared that competition from Canada would ruin them and that the new Canadian tariff on imported foreign goods, especially from the United States, would increase the cost of living in the colony. In 1865, Tilley's government fell to the opposition party led by Albert J. Smith. Confederation was dead—at least, for a while.

New Brunswick's rejection of Confederation forced Nova Scotia Premier Charles Tupper to postpone Nova Scotia's vote on the issue. As in New Brunswick, many merchants and bankers in Nova Scotia feared competition from Canada. As well, with the British navy stationed in Halifax, there was no reason to fear American invasion, and thus no need for the protection Confederation might afford them.

Newfoundland's merchants also feared that a union would hurt trade and increase the cost of imported goods. Neither railways nor defence were of interest to the Newfoundlanders—they would be far separated from the proposed railway and the British navy was sufficient to protect them against threats from the United States. The capital of the new union would also be too far away for Newfoundlanders to have much influence on government policies.

Although the Quebec Conference largely ignored the Island's political and economic needs, at the conclusion of the Quebec Conference the Island delegation was divided. John Hamilton Gray, Thomas Heath Haviland, William Henry Pope, and Edward Whelan favoured Confederation. Whelan, for example, argued, "a union will relieve us from the provoking intermeddling of the Colonial Office in our local legislation...."

George Coles, Archibald MacDonald, and Edward Palmer disagreed. After years of economic struggle, the Island economy was finally prospering, and they saw no urgent need for change. The reciprocity agreement the British government had signed with the United States in 1854 had opened new markets for Island produce; the local population had risen from forty-seven thousand people in 1841 to eighty-one thousand in 1861; and new communities were emerging in every part of the Island.

Accompanying this economic growth was a growing pride and sense of identity. Although religion, politics, and class differences divided Islanders, their separation from the rest of the mainland colonies gave them a sense of uniqueness. This newfound sense of identity caused many Islanders to wonder how five representatives in distant Ottawa could possibly protect their interests. Thus, the Island government vetoed Confederation by a combined vote of thirty-six to five in 1865, and thirty-four to seven the following year.

The Tide Turns
When the American Civil War ended in 1865, the Northern Army released thousands of soldiers. Fenians, Irish-Americans who wanted Britain to free Ireland, comprised some of these ex-soldiers. The Fenians planned to capture British North America and trade it to Britain in return for Ireland's freedom.

In 1866, the Fenians mounted attacks on New Brunswick and several places in the Province of Canada. Except for a small moment of glory at the battle of Ridgeway, these raids were utter failures. However, they convinced many people in New Brunswick of the danger from the south, and the need for railways to transport troops and a larger union for better defence. As a result, New Brunswick voters elected Tilley's pro-Confederation government in 1866. Now that New Brunswick had accepted Confederation, Premier Tupper acted quickly. He bribed several members of the New Brunswick legislature who had opposed Confederation, and, with the British government's help, he convinced the Nova Scotian legislature to agree to a scheme of union in which its rights and interests were ensured.

Since the colonies needed Britain's permission to change their constitutions, sixteen delegates from the Canadas, Nova Scotia, and New Brunswick met in London, England, in December 1866 to finalize Confederation. There, Tilley and Tupper made one last attempt to win over the Island by promising the Islanders $800,000 to purchase the holdings of the absentee landlords if they joined Confederation. The British government attempted to coerce the Islanders into changing their minds by threatening not to protect the colony against attack and warning that they would be forced to pay the lieutenant-governor's salary if they didn't join. Prince Edward Island refused to give in to such blackmail, especially as it was still upset with Britain's refusal to solve the land problems.

The law that created Canada, the British North America Act, received royal assent on March 29, 1867, and was implemented on July 1, 1867, when Canada became the first dominion in the British Empire. There were no ringing declarations of independence in Canada as there had been in the United States when the Americans broke away from the British Empire in 1776. In fact, Great Britain still retained control over Canada's foreign affairs, defence, international trade, and constitution.

The day the British North America Act received royal assent, citizens of the newly united Canada celebrated. Church bells rang, cannons boomed their salutes, fireworks lit the sky, bands played "God Save the Queen," and Union Jacks lined the streets as the newly knighted Sir John A. Macdonald walked to the parliament buildings in Ottawa to become Canada's first prime minister.

The Island Enters Confederation

The next attempt to change Islanders' minds about Confederation came in 1869. A year earlier, Benjamin Butler, a member of the government of the United States, had visited Prince Edward Island to discuss a trade agreement to replace the lapsed reciprocity treaty between the Island and the United States. The meetings went well, and the American delegation presented a favourable report to congress. However, under pressure from the Colonial Office, the Island

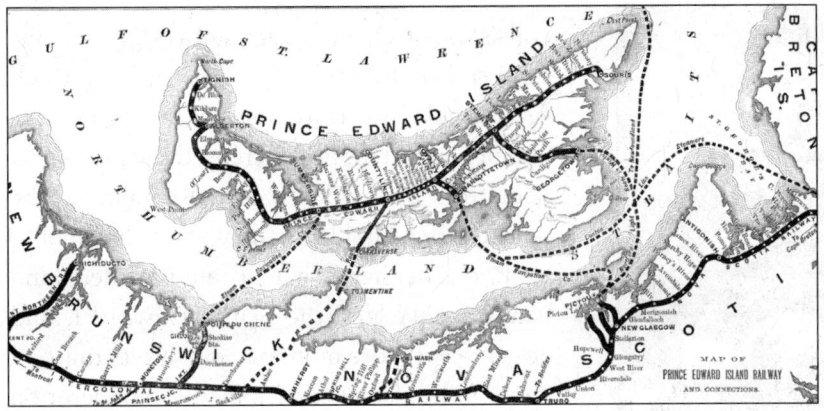

Railway lines on the Island and in nearby parts of New Brunswick and Nova Scotia, 1884. The Island railway brought growth to the towns along its line.

legislature agreed not to pursue a trade deal with the United States without British permission.

Prime Minister Macdonald feared that the United States might parlay economic agreements into political control and use Prince Edward Island as a military base. The colony was also in a strategic position to control the fisheries and smuggle goods into Canada. To prevent this, in December 1869, Macdonald offered the Island more tax money and passenger steamer service to the mainland in return for the Island joining Confederation, and renewed Canada's promise of $800,000 to purchase the remaining absentee landlord holdings if the Island joined. The Island's Liberal government under Premier Robert Haythorne rejected the offer as insufficient.

Two years later, the Island government decided to build a railway spanning the Island from Alberton to Georgetown. It would be the first railway on the Island, and the idea was very popular. Everyone would prosper—or so many people believed. Construction workers would be hired, factories would be built, and farmers would be able to transport their crops to the towns more rapidly.

The terms of the construction contract established a fixed price per mile, but set no limit on the number of miles to be constructed. Since every village wanted to be connected to the main line, railway branch lines soon crisscrossed the Island. One-third of the line

James Colledge Pope, premier of Prince Edward Island (1865-1867, 1870, 1873). Pope resigned as premier in 1873 and later became a member of Parliament and cabinet minister in Ottawa.

consisted of curves, with an average of one train station for every five kilometres of track. As a result, the railway cost far more than initially expected, and increased the provincial debt from $250,000 to over $4 million. The railway's bond holders soon wanted their money back, but neither Great Britain nor the Island banks would lend the Prince Edward Island government more money to pay off its railroad debts unless the Island joined Confederation and thereby improved its credit.

Thus, in February 1873, Island Premier Robert Haythorne travelled to Ottawa and negotiated terms for entering Confederation. The proposed deal was then put before Island voters in a general election. James Pope, who promised to fight for even better terms, won the election and led another delegation to Ottawa to negotiate a new deal. After holding out for six years, the Island received a guarantee that Ottawa would assume its debts and liabilities; operate and maintain the Island railway; provide an "efficient and continuous" telegraphic and steamship communication with the mainland; grant the Island six members of Parliament (the population had increased since 1864); and supply $800,000 to buy the landlords' property. This new agreement passed through the Island legislature with only two nay votes.

On July 1, 1873, Prince Edward Island joined Canada. Buildings throughout Charlottetown were decorated with flags and streamers, ships in the harbour were festooned with ribbon, and church bells peeled to mark the occasion. However, Confederation was still not overly popular with Islanders, as the following account from the Charlottetown *Patriot* indicates: "...among the people who thronged the streets there was no enthusiasm.... After the reading of the Proclamation was concluded, the gentlemen on the balcony gave a cheer, but the three persons below...responded never a word."

ROBERT HARRIS: ARTIST

At the end of the nineteenth century, Robert Harris was the most renowned portrait painter in Canada. In 1883, the Canadian government decided to have a painting made of the Fathers of Confederation to celebrate the twentieth anniversary of the Charlottetown Conference, and it selected Robert Harris as the artist. Harris agreed to take on the commission, but soon discovered that the job was more difficult than he had originally thought. Several of the politicians who had attended the conference had died, and the others were twenty years older. Determined to be as accurate as possible, Harris collected photographs of those who had died and sent questionnaires to people who had known the deceased politicians asking about the delegates' height, hair colour, facial hair, eyes, clothes, and even the size of their hands. Harris met with those Fathers of Confederation who were still living.

Robert Harris

The painting, which took Harris a year to finish, brought him instant fame. It was hung in the Parliament Buildings at Ottawa and later appeared on several Canadian postage stamps and was reproduced for classrooms across the country.

When the Parliament Buildings burnt down in 1916, Harris's painting was destroyed. All that remains of Harris's painting today are copies and the charcoal sketch from which he made the original.

Robert Harris's painting of the Fathers of Confederation

CHAPTER NINE
Prosperity and Decline

The late nineteenth century was a tumultuous time on the Island, economically speaking. Although small-scale manufacturing was booming at mid-century, Island factories were unable to compete with the cheaper goods from central Canadian factories and the Island's manufacturing sector declined steadily after Confederation. Over-harvesting weakened both the timber industry and the fishery, although the later was rescued by the emergence of the lobster-canning industry. The prosperous shipbuilding industry disappeared completely. By the end of the century, the Island's economy had changed dramatically, and its "golden age" had come to an end.

The Age of Wood, Wind, and Sail
Prince Edward Island was prosperous in the mid-nineteenth century. This was the age of wood, wind, and water and almost every harbour echoed with the sounds of shipbuilding. The Island was perfectly suited to shipbuilding—it had plenty of deep, sheltered harbours and a good supply of nearby timber. By the 1830s, shipbuilding yards were scattered over the colony, and in the next sixty years approximately 3,700 vessels were constructed in more than 170 locations. Islanders built more ships per capita between the 1830s and 1890s than any other British colony and made more money sailing and selling ships than they did exporting agricultural goods.

Island shipbuilders such as Lemuel Cambridge, William Ellis, James Peake, James Yeo, James Duncan, J. C. Pope, and William Heard gained a reputation for their well-built vessels. The most commonly constructed boats on the Island at the time were schooners, barques, and brigantines, but not every type of sailing ship was built in every port. Shipyards in Mount Stewart concentrated on brigantines; those in Grand River and Port Hill preferred barques and barquentines;

Shipping at Montague, P. E. Island

SAILS AND RIGGING

Sailing vessels are usually described by how their sails are arranged (or rigged). The two main styles of rigging are square and fore-and-aft. If a mast is square-rigged, it means the sails are at right angles to the keel. Fore-and-aft rigs have sails running the same direction as the keel. Depending on their intended uses, Islanders built square-rigged ships for the open sea, or fore-and-aft rigged ships for navigating closer to shore.

and shipyards in Souris and New Glasgow concentrated on schooners. In general, Island vessels tended to be smaller than those constructed in either Nova Scotia or New Brunswick, and were designed to carry large quantities of goods.

Building a Ship

Island timber was usually cut in the winter and hauled out of the woods by teams of horses or oxen. Shipbuilding began with the approach of spring, and Island shipyards came alive with the sound of axes thudding into wood, bringing prosperity to nearby villages. Summerside, for example, owed its growth to shipbuilding, and by 1871, it was second in size to Charlottetown.

Many Island-built vessels were filled with local squared timber and sailed to Great Britain. There, both the timber and the ship were sold. Other vessels were sold in Nova Scotia, New Brunswick, and Newfoundland. Some Island shipbuilders kept their vessels and used them to carry potatoes, oats, wheat, lumber, fish, and livestock to Newfoundland, Nova Scotia, the United States, and the West Indies.

JAMES YEO: OPPORTUNIST

James Yeo was one of the Island's most successful shipbuilders. Although he was born into a poor family in Cornwall, England, in 1789, by the time he died at the age of seventy-nine, he was the richest man on Prince Edward Island. The first thirty years of Yeo's life were filled with unhappiness. His wife, who bore him three sons, died in 1818. As a result, Yeo, a labourer and carter, began to drink heavily, and soon lost his job. Yeo later remarried, and he and his wife, Damaris, immigrated to Port Hill, Prince Edward Island, where he took a job working for a British businessman named Thomas Burnard. Yeo managed Burnard's lumber gangs and helped with his general stores and shipbuilding business.

James Yeo

During the next two decades Yeo combined hard work, intelligence, and ruthlessness to make a fortune. When Burnard died in 1826, Yeo apparently pretended he was Burnard's agent and collected money from those who were in debt to Burnard. He used this money to go into business—setting himself up as a lumber dealer and storekeeper in Port Hill, and purchasing a small schooner. He later pretended to own much of the land in Prince County and, it was said, sent his employees there to cut down valuable timber. Because many of the tenants were illiterate and couldn't read their land deeds, Yeo was able to get away with this deceit.

Yeo's family helped with his businesses. His wife and their five daughters managed the Port Hill store—selling the tobacco, salt, tea, rum, nails, shoes, molasses, meat, cloth, rope, and saws that Yeo's ships imported from Great Britain and Nova Scotia. His sons bought lumber, oats, livestock, and salted cod, which they exported to Great Britain in Yeo's ships. His two youngest sons and his sons-in-law built over two hundred vessels.

Many of these ships sailed unfinished to England, where they were completed at the family's shipyard, which was managed by Yeo's oldest son. With his family's help, James Yeo became the most prolific shipbuilder on the Island.

As he became more powerful, Yeo developed an interest in politics. He was elected to the assembly in 1839, serving on and off until 1863, and he later became a member of the executive council. By the 1860s, Yeo was so wealthy that the Island government approached him for loans and it was rumoured that his employees earned more money than the total government revenue. Although he was not a popular man, by the time James Yeo died of pneumonia in 1868, he had done much to develop the Island's economy.

Fish and Lobster

At mid-century the Island's fishing industry was undeveloped. Many Islanders could not afford to invest in the wharves and vessels that were necessary to compete with other colonies' fishing fleets. Although the Convention of 1818 between the American and the British governments forbade American ships from fishing within three miles of the British North American coast, many Islanders wanted to remove the three-mile limit and other trade restrictions in hopes that Prince Edward Island would become a base for American ships and Island exports.

The 1854 Reciprocity Treaty between British North America and the United States eliminated the three-mile fishing limit. When the Island government allowed non-British subjects to own Island land and to acquire coastal property for "business enterprises" in 1858, American money flowed north to finance fishing operations all over the Island. The number of registered fishing companies multiplied from five in 1850 to eighty-nine in 1861, and by 1864, the fishing industry was responsible for approximately eighteen percent of all Island exports. Most of these exports, including dried cod, salt herring, gaspereau, mackerel, and fish oil, went directly to the United States.

At mid-century, there was no economical method to keep lobsters alive until they reached the market. Unlike cod or mackerel, lobsters could not be dried, salted, or pickled. At this time, lobsters were found in such abundance that all that was required to catch them

BEACONSFIELD: A SHIPBUILDER'S HOME

Beaconsfield

In 1877, James Peake, one of the Island's wealthiest shipbuilders, hired architect William Critchlow Harris to design a house that would reflect his economic and social standing. Peake built this elegant Victorian home, which boasted a mansard roof, elaborate gingerbread trim, and expansive lawns, overlooking Charlottetown Harbour. Constructed at a then-astronomical cost of fifty thousand dollars, the house, which was named Beaconsfield, had twenty-five rooms and eight fireplaces, two of which were marble.

In 1882, an economic recession and the theft of funds from the Bank of Prince Edward Island, of which Peake was a director, forced him to sell Beaconsfield. Thirty years later, Beaconsfield became a refuge for young women working in Charlottetown or attending Prince of Wales College. It subsequently became a residence for student nurses. In 1970, the Prince Edward Island Heritage Foundation assumed control of Beaconsfield, restored the building to its earlier glory, and opened it for visitors.

Fishing craft in Souris. Large fleets of American and Nova Scotian fishing vessels landed in Souris every summer in the late nineteenth century for provisioning. Souris vessels exported oats, dried and pickled fish, and potatoes.

in shallow water or at low tide were wooden tongs; in some areas, it was simply a matter of dropping a net into the water and waiting several minutes. Lobsters were so cheap and plentiful in the mid-nineteenth century that they were even used as fertilizer. The advent of lobster canning procedures in the 1870s, however, changed this crustacean into a delicacy.

As soon as the lobsters were landed at the cannery's wharf, the catch was weighed and carted to the boiler room where the lobsters were cooked in huge cast-iron kettles. The cooked lobsters were then washed, cooled, and placed on an assembly line. "Crackers" broke the claw and tail shells; "shakers," who were usually women, extracted the meat; "pickers" squeezed the meat out of the legs; and "packers" stuffed the lobster meat into cans lined with oiled paper and topped them up with brine. Some canneries saved the green tomally (liver) for lobster paste. The cans were then sealed using a foot-operated soldering machine and sterilized. Next, a small hole was made in the top of each can to allow the steam to escape. Then the cans were resealed with solder, boiled in sea water to create a vacuum, and packed in wooden cases. It took about two hundred pounds of uncooked lobster to fill a forty-eight-pound case of canned

Robert Harris's Acadian Women in Cannery, at Canoe Cove, 1880. *The Harris family owned a cannery in Canoe Cove.*

lobster. The canneries shipped the bulk of their product to the United Kingdom and France, with smaller quantities going to Germany, Belgium, Austria, and Russia.

Between 1873 and 1883, the value of the Island's lobster fishery increased from $218,000 to $2 million. The number of canneries, which were located near almost every harbour and bay, reached 246 in 1900, with Murray Harbour at the centre of the industry. The lobster fishery employed more than 3,100 workers on a seasonal basis in 1900 and spawned several spin-off industries, such as can-making. Cannery jobs were highly sought-after, especially by women, whose choices of paid employment were limited. In the cannery, they performed traditional female tasks such as cooking and cleaning and earned less than half of what male workers made.

The first signs that the lobster stock was declining began to appear in the mid-1880s. In order to protect the lobster population, in 1889 the federal government established two lobster fishing seasons and made it illegal to keep lobsters whose eggs were attached. Shortly

The Charlottetown Condensed Milk Factory, 1908

afterwards, the government began requiring lobster fishers to obtain licenses, pay a per-trap fee, and keep only the large lobsters. However, these regulations were poorly enforced and the lobster population continued to decline.

Island Agriculture

Agriculture was by far the largest industry on the Island in the late nineteenth century. The Island's soil and climate were ideal for raising horses, sheep, cattle, and hogs, and for growing wheat, oats, barley, rye, beans, peas, and—of course—world-famous Prince Edward Island potatoes.

In the second half of the century, farmers began using mussel mud as a fertilizer. Although there were mussel shells in the mud, it was actually the large amount of oyster shells that provided the valuable lime that fertilized the soil. The shell beds were usually about two metres deep, although in St. Peter's Bay they were up to ten metres deep. Despite its advantages, mussel mud was not used very much until the 1860s because it was too difficult to shovel out of the water. The invention of a horse-powered digging machine in the 1860s solved this problem. Dressed in warm layers of winter wool, farmers gathered

Silver foxes

on the ice with their sleds near the large wooden mud-diggers. In North River, South West River, Brudenell, and St. Peter's Bay, as many as a hundred farmers huddled in the cold, waiting to get their sleighs loaded with fertilizer. In 1916, the government began to load mussel mud from St. Peter's Bay onto railway flatcars and deliver it to inland areas that were too far from the coast to obtain the fertilizer. These "mud special" trains continued to operate until the 1920s, when artificial fertilizers became more readily available.

By the end of the nineteenth century, 1.2 million of the Island's 1.4 million acres were devoted to farming. Many farms were committed to the dairy industry, which produced more than half of a million dollars annually and was responsible for another Island moniker—"The Denmark of Canada." Despite the Island's economic reliance on agriculture, however, it wasn't until 1902 that the provincial government established a department of agriculture.

Silver Foxes

The development of fox farming at the turn of the century brought much-needed money to the province. In the early 1800s, Islanders Charles Dalton and Robert Oulton often went hunting together to capture live red foxes, which they sold to American fox-hunting clubs. The beautiful pelt of the rarer black fox, however, was much more valuable. The guard hairs of the black fox are tipped with silver—hence the term "silver fox."

Dalton and Oulton realized they would earn a fortune if they could breed silver foxes in captivity. After several years of experimenting, the two entrepreneurs recreated the animals' natural lair at their Island ranch near Alberton, and captured male and female black foxes to breed them. In 1896, Dalton and Oulton's fox-breeding program was finally successful—their fortunes were secured.

The partners sought to keep their success a secret—they did not even tell their wives and children about the details of the breeding. They hired a guard to protect the ranch grounds at night, and Dalton secretly mailed the pelts from a distant post office or sneaked out at night to send them by ship. Secrets, however, are hard to keep in a place as small as Prince Edward Island, and it was not long before other people in Prince County became interested in fox ranching.

In 1898, Silas Rayner, B. I. Rayner, Robert Tuplin, and James Gordon formed a partnership with Oulton and Dalton. The "Big Six," as they were called, agreed to keep their fox-breeding practices secret and limit the supply of pelts to keep prices high. When one of the members broke the monopoly by selling a pair of breeding foxes the next year, the fox boom began. Three years later, there were approximately three hundred fox ranches on the Island and the industry was valued at twenty million dollars. The silver fox industry continued to be an important contributor to the Island economy well into the twentieth century.

The Growth of Manufacturing

Agricultural growth evolved hand-in-glove with industrial production on the Island. With manufacturing, as with agriculture, the Island

ROBERT TINSON HOLMAN: MERCHANT

This 1932 postcard depicts Holman's department store in Summerside

The story of Robert T. Holman is fairly typical of the rise of the merchant class on the Island. Robert and his family emigrated from England to Saint John in 1819 and his father became involved in the shipping business. When his father's business failed, thirteen-year-old Robert left school and took several jobs in Saint John and Boston before moving to Prince Edward Island in 1850. During the next five years he worked for various family members in Charlottetown, St. Eleanors, and Summerside before opening his own store in Summerside.

Robert had a genius for commerce. His store was always orderly and neat, and he looked after the smallest details. When Robert made a promise, he would rather lose money than break his word, and he allowed customers who were unhappy with their goods to either exchange them or get their money back—a benefit few other stores offered. Holman kept in close touch with Island farmers, which helped him decide which goods to buy for his store.

Robert's business savvy paid off. By 1893, he owned a three-storey brick building, nine sailing vessels, a large freight house, a warehouse, several wharves, a meat and poultry cannery, a lobster factory, and several waterfront lots. He was one of the first merchants to export lobsters and later became a shareholder in the Summerside Electric Company. When Robert T. Holman died, he had created one of the best family-run businesses in the Maritimes. His sons, Harry T. and James Le Roy, later enlarged the family empire by adding oysters, farm machinery, and fox farming.

was generally self-sufficient. By 1871, there were more than five hundred carding, wool, grist, saw, fulling, dressing, and shingle mills on Prince Edward Island. There were also a number of small factories, which produced a variety of goods, such as leather, butter, wheels, furniture, shoes, horse-drawn buggies, tobacco, beer, cheese, fish oil, bricks, sleighs, clothes, pianos, mowing machines, and iron plows. It was during the late nineteenth century that such prominent Island business people as R. T. Holman, M. F. Schurman, J. C. Pope, David Rogers, John L. Mackinnon, and John Linkletter got their start.

Financing the Economy

Because there were no banks on the Island until the mid-nineteenth century, Islanders used a wide array of coins from Spain, Great Britain, United States, Mexico, Peru, France, Ireland, and elsewhere. Each coin's value was based on the amount of precious metal it contained. The only paper money used on the Island at this time consisted of government treasury notes and local merchants' private bills.

The lack of banks on the Island was particularly hard on importers and exporters. To do business, they required large amounts of credit to tide them over the gap between purchase and sale. Retail merchants had to await sales before repaying their loans, and farmers required credit to operate their farms until their crops matured. Because of the high demand for credit, private lenders often charged usurious interest rates.

By the 1850s, the economy had grown sufficiently to warrant the establishment of a bank, and several prominent businessmen worked together to establish the Bank of Prince Edward Island, which was incorporated in 1856. It was an immediate success. By providing credit at reasonable rates, issuing its own currency, and directing the community's surplus funds into the hands of entrepreneurs, the bank provided a healthy climate for business transactions.

Additional banks soon followed, and by the 1870s the banks had extended their influence throughout the Island. Banks established on the Island during the late nineteenth century included the Bank of Prince Edward Island (1856–1882), the Farmers' Bank of Rustico (1864–1894),

A Bank of Prince Edward Island five-dollar note. Each bank issued its own currency.

the Union Bank (1864–1883), the Bank of Summerside (1866–1901), and the Merchants Bank of Prince Edward Island (1871–1906).

Unfortunately, Island banks were not well-suited to survive a long recession such as the one that plagued the Island in the post-Confederation years. One of the banks' major weaknesses was that most bank directors were uninterested in banking as a profession. They became directors for its advantages: dividends, an annual honorarium, and easy access to credit. At least one director admitted that he did not understand double-entry accounting—making it virtually impossible for him to examine the bank's books as required. The directors thus left the day-to-day banking operations to the cashiers, often without adequate supervision.

In 1857, this oversight almost destroyed the Bank of Prince Edward Island; in 1882, it ruined the bank. The second failure was largely due to the misguided dealings of Joseph Brecken, the bank's cashier. On November 21, 1881, Brecken fled to New Brunswick, explaining what he had done and why in a letter to his wife:

> *I know what people will say about me, I deserve it all and plead guilty. Where loan customers got the thin [edge] of the wedge in, I had to go on advancing [money] in order...to get the whole monies due the bank back without loss. This every person promised*

to do. I had to keep these facts from the directors or I would have been dismissed from the bank. I therefore commenced my downward course by telling lies and ended by making false accounts.

When the bank's borrowers defaulted on their loans, the Bank of Prince Edward Island filed for bankruptcy. This led to a loss of confidence in the banking system as a whole, and the following year the Union Bank amalgamated with the larger Bank of Nova Scotia in Halifax and soon closed its offices in Summerside and Montague. In 1906, the Merchants Bank of Prince Edward Island—which had failed in part because its directors had siphoned the bank's money off for dubious business ventures—amalgamated with the Canadian Bank of Commerce.

These changes were part of a general movement in the Canadian financial sector that saw the amalgamation of local banks with larger banks headquartered in Montreal and Toronto. Although the movement from local to national banks brought financial stability, it also reduced availability, as the number of Islanders served per branch declined from 9,900 in 1881 to 13,600 ten years later—the worst ratio in the nation. In addition, it became much harder for Islanders to borrow money from the banks, which preferred to lend it to Western Canadian projects that offered greater potential returns.

Mass Exodus
With the advent of steel and steam near the end of the century, the Island's "golden age" came to an end. Between 1881 and 1901, the number of factories in Charlottetown declined from 198 to 31 as demand for their products waned and the number of factory workers fell from 1,005 to 558.

The most obvious evidence of the hard times was the steady decline in the Island's population. Despairing of finding employment, approximately thirty thousand Islanders left for New England and the Prairies between 1870 and 1900. The population finally bottomed out at eighty-six thousand in 1924, after numbering more than one hundred thousand at the beginning of the century. Although out-migration relieved the province of its surplus labour, it tended to be the young, educated people who left the Island, creating an older, less entrepreneurial populace.

While Islanders were deserting the region, several million immigrants began pouring into the prosperous Canadian West, and the percentage of Canada's population living on the Island fell from 2.5 in 1881 to 0.8 in 1941. This population loss resulted in a commensurate reduction in political clout as the Island's number of members of Parliament, which was based on its proportion of the country's population, fell to five in 1892 and to four in 1904. When it appeared that this number would drop to three, the province vigorously protested. In 1915, the Island was guaranteed at least four members in the House of Commons.

CHAPTER TEN
Island Life at the Turn of the Twentieth Century

Despite the economic difficulties they were facing, Islanders ended the nineteenth century in an optimistic mood. In 1902, the Charlottetown *Patriot* reported, "At the beginning of the century the Island was forest primeval while today, city, towns and villages flourish, and the 'million acre farm' is thickly dotted with substantial homesteads, well tilled fields and bursting barns.... We have great hope and unbounded faith in the future for Canada for Prince Edward Island."

The turn of the twentieth century was certainly an exciting time to be alive. Kodak's new hand-held box camera sold for only one dollar. "You press the button, we do the rest," the advertisement boasted. The most popular home entertainment device was the phonograph, which played one-minute-long wax cylinders. In sports, basketball had begun to allow dribbling, and par had been adopted for keeping score in golf.

However, the automobile was the invention that inaugurated the greatest changes at the turn of the century. Islanders were initially wary of this new invention. In September 1906, L. M. Montgomery expressed her disapproval of automobiles, remarking, "Do you know I was nearly run over by an *automobile* last night! Automobiles in Cavendish! There is no such thing as solitude left on earth!"

The first automobiles were started by hand-cranks, were noisy and slow, broke down frequently, and got flat tires every few miles. Since they had no windshields, the dust from the unpaved Island roads was a problem for drivers and passengers, and Island women often wore veils and long coats called "dusters" to protect their clothes while riding in an automobile. Considered by many Islanders to be a menace, or a fad for the rich or the stupid, automobiles (all seven

The Masonic Lodge Opera House, Grafton Street, Charlottetown, 1894. It later became the Prince Edward Theatre.

of them on the Island at the time) were banned from the Island in 1908. Prince Edward Island thus became the only provincial or state jurisdiction ever to enact a total ban on automobiles. Anyone caught driving a car was sentenced to six months in jail or a fine of five hundred dollars.

The advent of electricity also greatly affected the Island way of life at the turn of the century. Prior to the introduction of electric lights on the major Charlottetown streets, residents carried lanterns to light their way. In 1863, the editor of the Charlottetown *Examiner* wrote that street lights "will be absolutely necessary during the long winter evenings to guide us over the puddles of mud and snow water, heaps of filth in the squares, dangerous crossings, and the still more dangerous sidewalks which are to be found in abundance in this favoured city of ours." However, streetlights were not erected on Charlottetown streets until 1887, and to save money, they were left unlit on moonlight nights.

The first telephone service on the Island was established in Charlottetown in 1885. Two years later, Summerside was connected, and in 1911 interprovincial calls were made possible via a submerged cable reaching from Wood Islands to Pictou, Nova Scotia. However, at 17.5 people per telephone in 1928, the Island had the lowest ratio in Canada.

Entertainment

Each Island community provided its own entertainment at the turn of the century. Strawberry festivals, basket socials, and tea and ice cream parties were frequent occurrences, and were often combined with such serious matters as political speeches and charity fundraising. In 1890, for example, the Souris Benevolent Irish Society held a fundraising tea party that promised good food, games, bowling, swings, hurdles, races, and a lecture on scientific farming. Other socials were just for fun, such as the 1882 railway employees' picnic, which advertised a day filled with foot races, standing-jump and hammer-throwing competitions, wheelbarrow races, a three-legged race, a potato race, a sword dance, Irish jigs, and Scottish hornpipes.

Agricultural fairs were the high point of the year in almost every village. Farmers paraded their prize animals and women competed for prizes for the best knitting, preserves, and baking. Everyone watched the horse and bicycle races. Manufacturers displayed their latest farm and household appliances.

Younger Island children enjoyed such activities as skipping, hide and seek, tag, and marbles. Older children and adults played kissing games, dominoes, crokinole, and checkers. By 1910, Islanders were enjoying shuffleboard, euchre, croquet, crossword puzzles, and watching silent films in the Charlottetown and Summerside

PRESERVE ME FROM PIE SOCIALS

Lucy Maud Montgomery wrote in her journal on April 4, 1899: "Preserve me from 'pie socials.' They are the abomination of desolation. The programme is only a pretence—the real business of the evening is selling the pies, attended by fearful excitement in the pit. An auctioneer, chosen for strength of lung and ability to crack dollar-coaxing jokes is selected, and the pies are auctioned off to the highest bidder, who shells out his cash, gets his pie, and is whisked upstairs by the powers that be to find the fair builder thereof and eat it with her."

theatres. The Prince Edward Theatre in Charlottetown offered a feature movie and three short films that ran continuously in the evening. Orchestra seating was ten cents and balcony seating was five cents.

Lawrence Doyle was one of the Island's best-known songwriters in the early twentieth century. Nicknamed "The Farmer Poet," Doyle specialized in gentle satire, and his lyrics poked fun at local people and situations. For example, one of his better-known songs, "The Picnic at Groshaut," tells the story of what happened when alcoholic cider was accidentally served at a local tea party instead of non-alcoholic cider.

MY FIRST BOOK: L. M. MONTGOMERY

Left: Lucy Maud Montgomery
Right: A cover image from a 1998 edition of Anne of Green Gables

Lucy Maud Montgomery was born in 1874 in the small Island village of Clifton (now New London), Prince Edward Island, where her father worked in a general store. When Montgomery was twenty-one months old, her mother died of tuberculosis. Her father, unable to raise a child on his own, moved to Saskatchewan, and Montgomery was sent to Cavendish to be raised by her mother's parents. Montgomery spent most of the next thirty-seven years in Cavendish.

After earning a teaching certificate at the Prince of Wales College in Charlottetown in 1893, Montgomery taught school in Bideford. From 1895 to 1896, she studied literature at Dalhousie University in Halifax before teaching at various Island schools. When her grandfather died in 1898, Montgomery left teaching—a career she had not enjoyed—and returned to Cavendish to take care of her grandmother and to write. In 1905, Montgomery scribbled the following idea for a story in her notebook: "Elderly couple apply to orphan asylum for a boy. By mistake a girl is sent to them." Montgomery wrote a novel based on this premise and set in Cavendish and submitted it to several publishers. After Montgomery's manuscript was rejected by five publishers, she tossed it in an old hat box and forgot about it.

Several years later, Montgomery found the manuscript, reread it, and sent it out again. Her first book, *Anne of Green Gables*, was finally published in 1908, and was an instant success. The success came as a complete surprise to her, and on the day she received her first copy back from the publisher she wrote, "My book came today, fresh from the publishers. I candidly confess that it was for me a proud, wonderful, thrilling moment. There in my hand lay the material realization of all the dreams and hopes and ambitions and struggles of my whole conscious existence—my first book! Not a great book at all—but mine, mine, mine—something to which I had given birth—something which, but for me, would never have existed."

Montgomery followed the success of *Anne of Green Gables* with three other novels before marrying Reverend Ewan Macdonald in 1911 and moving to Ontario with him. There, despite the demanding duties of being a minister's wife and the mother of two sons, Montgomery published another sixteen novels and maintained a prolific writing career. By the time she died in 1942, Montgomery had written twenty novels, five hundred short stories, five hundred poems, ten journals, a number of scrapbooks, and an autobiography.

Shortly after her death, Lucy Maud Montgomery was recognized by the Historic Sites and Monuments Board of Canada as being a person of national historic significance, and a monument and plaque were erected in her honour at Green Gables Heritage Place, the real-life setting of *Anne of Green Gables*, in Cavendish in 1948. Each year, more than half of the tourists to the Island come to Cavendish to visit the home of Anne Shirley, the heroine of *Anne of Green Gables*.

One hundred years after *Anne of Green Gables* was first published, Anne Shirley is still the best-known fictional character in Canadian history, and more people have read *Anne of Green Gables* than any other Canadian book.

Sports and Recreation

With the growth of urbanization on the Island in the late nineteenth century, athletics began to enjoy widespread popularity. Despite the long workdays, urban dwellers had specific periods of leisure time that reoccurred at regular intervals. This made it possible to schedule sporting competitions weeks and months ahead. The most popular sports on the Island in the late nineteenth century were rugby, track and field, cycling, and cricket. During the 1870s and 80s, Charlottetown's Phoenix cricket team competed against the best teams in the Maritimes. Baseball developed slower on the Island than elsewhere. It wasn't until 1889 that the first baseball team was formed in Charlottetown, and not until 1896 that the Island held its first provincial championship.

Organized sports on the Island owed much of their development to the Young Men's Christian Association, the Caledonia Club, and the Abegweit Athletic Club. The Abegweit Athletic Club, for example, fielded teams in hockey, rugby, baseball, tennis, and track and field. Between 1900 and 1912, thanks largely to Abegweit club members Bill Halpenny (Canadian pole-vault champion), James "Toby" MacMillan (Maritime sprint champion), and Michael Thomas (Maritime long-distance champion), the Abegweit club won the Maritime track and field championship nine times. Halpenny and Philip Blake McDonald (track) represented Canada in the Olympics—Halpenny in 1904 and 1912, and McDonald in 1924.

Between 1909 and 1912, Mi'kmaq athlete Michael Thomas of Lennox Island was the best distance runner in eastern Canada. Although Thomas did not begin racing until he was in his mid-twenties, he achieved instant success and was termed the "Island Longboat" in reference to the famous Six Nations' marathoner Tom Longboat, whose success

---

A TYPICAL BASEBALL CHALLENGE

In July 1891, the *Daily Examiner* printed the following challenge, which was typical of how baseball games were organized at this time: "The Pisquid Baseball Club intend holding a picnic on their grounds near Pisquid Station on Thursday, July 23 on which day they are prepared to meet and play any other nine on Prince Edward Island. If a match can be arranged it will take place at 2 o'clock on their grounds at Pisquid."

inspired Thomas to take up running. Thomas himself inspired such other Island Mi'kmaq runners as Barney Francis and John Paul.

Hockey was slower to gain popularity on the Island. In Ottawa, Governor-General Lord Stanley's children fell in love with hockey and convinced him to donate a trophy (the Stanley Cup) for the best team in Canada in 1892. At that time, goals had no nets, the players did not wear gloves, and the referee appeared in ordinary clothes. The seven-man teams (there was a "rover" position) played two halves and no substitutes were permitted. Goalies generally wore cricket pads and were penalized if they fell to the ice to stop the puck. Probably the most important difference from today was that it was illegal to pass the puck forward. This made for frequent stoppages of play and low-scoring games, which perhaps explain why hockey was not yet as popular as some other sports.

In an era when many people believed that African Canadians could not endure cold, possessed ankles too weak to skate well, and lacked intelligence, black communities formed the Colored Hockey League of the Maritimes in 1900. Charlottetown's West End Rangers, dressed in black jerseys and yellow-trimmed pants, defeated the New Glasgow Rovers for the Coloured Hockey Championship of the World in 1901.

Bicycling on the Island

In the last two decades of the century the invention of the inexpensive modern bicycle—with its diamond-shaped frame, equal-sized wheels, chain-and-sprocket drive, and pneumatic tires—provided cheap transportation, changed clothing styles, and helped emancipate women. Individuals, lovers, and families took advantage of the new freedom offered by the bicycle to go on picnics and ride through the countryside. Chaperones were the first casualties of the bicycle craze, and courtship and proper etiquette had to be revised. Instead of waist-pinching corsets and layers of petticoats and whalebone stiffeners, daring women wore bloomers (a voluminous type of pants that exposed the ankle), although the majority of women adopted shortened riding skirts with knee-high garters. Male cyclists preferred knickerbockers and coarse, loose-fitting sweaters.

A group of cyclists stop to pose for a photo near Langley Beach.

Bicycle races were a regular feature of Island life at the turn of the century. Although the invention of the modern bicycle had made cycling easier, there was still no shortage of accidents during bicycle races. In 1898, the Charlottetown *Patriot* provided the following description of one such race:

> *As usual, accidents were quite common. Mr. Moore collided with a cow, which injured the fork of his wheel and impeded his speed afterwards. Mr. Haszard was unfortunate to break his handle-bars before leaving and had to borrow one. Mr. Duchemin when coming down the first hill struck a stone and was thrown from his wheel and rendered unable to take any further active part in the race.... Afterwards, there was an ice-cream and strawberry banquet, followed by speeches and a feast.*

Charlottetown-born Byron Richard Brown used his cycling skills to win multiple provincial and Maritime cycling titles. Following his cycling career, Byron captained several Abegweit rugby teams to the provincial championships.

The Minto *caught in the ice*

Crossing the Northumberland Strait

One of the reasons Islanders agreed to Confederation in 1873 was Canada's promise to provide "efficient and continuous communication" between the Island and the mainland. The first ferry provided by the Canadian government was the *Albert* (1875). Unfortunately, it was made mostly of wood and couldn't break through the thick winter ice. Although the next steamboat, the *Northern Light* (1876), was steel-hulled, it also was not strong enough to fight the heavy winter ice, and averaged only twenty-one round trips a winter.

The *Stanley* (1888) was a big improvement. Although this steel icebreaker averaged seventy-nine round trips per winter, it was still subject to the perils of winter. In 1890, for example, it was unable to make the crossing for forty-three consecutive days because the ice was too thick. The *Minto*, which commenced service in 1899, fared better. It could cut through twenty-eight centimetres of solid ice; if the ice was thicker than this, the captain could drive the ferry onto the ice to crush it with the boat's weight. If the ice still did not break, the ferry became stranded on the ice and the passengers were forced to walk to the nearest shore. Neither the *Stanley* nor the *Minto* was permitted to leave port in the winter without provisions for two months.

The *Prince Edward Island*, which came into service in 1918, was the first ferry capable of carrying railway cars and automobiles.

To Drink or Not to Drink

The Island's temperance movement dated back to pioneer days, when taverns dotted the countryside. Presbyterian minister Robert Patterson established the first temperance society in 1831 in Centreville to encourage people to drink in moderation. It was quickly followed by such organizations as the Independent Order of Good Templars and the Women's Christian Temperance Union. Later, temperance organizations moved from approving moderate use of beers and wine (but not spirits) to total abstinence from all alcoholic beverages, and from attempting to win converts by the use of moral arguments to demanding government legislation prohibiting all alcohol consumption, except that needed for sacramental and medicinal purposes.

The Canada Temperance Act of 1878 allowed each municipality to decide by majority vote whether liquor could be sold within its boundaries. Except for Charlottetown, which had one tavern for every 124 citizens in 1894, most Island communities voted in favour of prohibition.

Although Charlottetown's mayor, William Dawson, recommended that the best prevention was a liberal use of the cat-of-nine-tails or street labour with a ball and chain, prohibition did not deter people from drinking. Alcohol passed easily from wet to dry areas and making moonshine was both a popular and a lucrative enterprise. In 1901, the Island became the first province to enforce total prohibition. Alcohol was permitted only for medicinal, industrial, and sacramental purposes. However, Islanders could purchase beer with an alcohol content under 2.75 percent, and, until 1923, they could import it from other provinces.

CONVICTIONS FOR BREACH OF CHARLOTTETOWN BY-LAWS, 1912

Drunkenness:	215
Fast driving:	12
Corner loafing:	5
Disorderly on street:	7
Insulting and abusive language:	3
Spitting on sidewalks:	5
Assault and battery:	19
Larceny:	7
Breach of the Prohibition Act:	29

A Homogeneous Island

With ninety-seven percent of its population born in Canada, Prince Edward Island was the most ethnically homogeneous province in the country at the turn of the century. The vast majority of Islanders were of European descent. Of the 103,000 Islanders at the turn of the century, 41,750 were Scottish; 24,000 were English; 21,900 were Irish; and 13,870 were French. The next largest groups were German (710), Mi'kmaq (254), Dutch (240), and African-Canadian (141).

One of the largest non-British ethnic groups to immigrate to the Island at the turn of the century was of Lebanese origin. Many Christian Lebanese families—and sometimes whole villages—left Lebanon in the late nineteenth century to avoid Turkish persecution. The first Lebanese settlers began to arrive in the 1880s. Many young Lebanese immigrants became "pack peddlers"—merchants who travelled from farm to farm selling everything from tea to trousers to those families who seldom got to town. Although the farmers were at first wary of these strangers, they soon looked forward to the peddlers' visits, and sometimes offered them food and lodging. Through hard work, many of these merchants earned enough money to open small stores, some of which still exist today.

There continued to be a small African-Canadian population on the Island at the turn of the twentieth century. Most of the 141 African Canadians on the Island in 1901 lived in Charlottetown's "Bog" area. When this district was razed for a redevelopment project in 1903, many black Islanders left for the United States. By 1911, there were only 81 black people left on the Island.

The first Chinese immigrant arrived in Charlottetown in July 1891. Twenty years later, the Island's Chinese population had grown to six: all young, single males, who worked in the laundry business in Charlottetown. Shortly after the first Chinese men arrived in Charlottetown, a letter to the editor of the Charlottetown *Examiner* indicated the prejudiced attitudes some Islanders held toward the Chinese immigrants: "Sir, -- A few days ago we noticed on the street a Chinaman who, *The Examiner* said, had come for the purpose of starting a laundry. If this be true, is it not the right time for the citizens of Charlottetown to say, in emphatic terms, whether they need any of these people or not? ...Encourage this man, and inside of one month you will have a dozen of them." The author went on to state that the presence of the Chinese men was "undesirable," and that they would soon displace white workers from their jobs.

Island and Canadian prejudices were also evident in the treatment of the Mi'kmaq. When Prince Edward Island entered Confederation in 1873, the federal government assumed political control of the Island's Mi'kmaq population. Approximately three hundred Mi'kmaq lived on the Island at this time, mainly in Georgetown, Orwell, Rocky Point, Cascumpeque, Summerside, and the Lennox Island and Morell reserves. They survived by hunting geese in the spring; fishing and digging shellfish in the summer; and making axe handles, baskets, and oars in the winter to sell to nearby farmers. Aboriginal Peoples struggled to preserve their culture in the face of official government policy to assimilate them. Virtually neglected by the federal government, most Island Mi'kmaq lived from hand to mouth in squalid conditions.

The Acadians' Struggle to Survive
Prior to 1860, most Island Acadians lived together in their own communities and generally avoided contact with English-speaking people, which helped them preserve their culture and traditions. Since Acadian children were instructed almost solely in French, most Acadians could not speak English. In 1863, the government sought to impose uniform standards across the province, abolishing subsidies to Acadian teachers who did not meet the Board of Education's educational requirements and ending the requirement that they be able to speak and write French. In 1877, the Board of Education mandated that all schools be non-denominational, which meant that most Acadian French textbooks were banned from provincial schools for being religious. Many Acadian teachers and Roman Catholic priests, including Father Georges-Antoine Belcourt, fought against this attempt to destroy Acadian culture.

FATHER BELCOURT

Out of Fields Come Dreams *by Karen Gallant, which depicts Father Georges-Antoine Belcourt watching over the Farmers' Bank and the Acadians of Rustico*

In the fall of 1859, Father Georges-Antoine Belcourt arrived in Rustico to serve this Acadian parish, which was chronically short of francophone priests. Father Belcourt, then fifty-six years old, had worked for twenty-eight years as a missionary among the Aboriginal peoples in Manitoba and Minnesota. On arriving in Rustico, he noted the extreme economic hardships of the inhabitants, who were in debt to the landlords, and immediately set to work to improve the Acadians' quality of life.

Father Belcourt established the Catholic Institute of Rustico, which met regularly to present lectures on economics, farming, science, and geography. He used the institute to begin such projects as the Farmer's Bank of Rustico, a co-operative bank that would become the forerunner of the credit union movement in North America. Belcourt hoped that by running their own bank, Acadian farmers would learn proper business methods, and be able to borrow money at reasonable rates, pay their rent, and eventually buy new farms as well as maintain a spirit of independence. In this, his hopes were only partially realized.

To train bilingual teachers and thus preserve the French language, Belcourt established a French high school, hired a teacher and musician from Quebec, and worked in the school until a sufficient number of good teachers were available. Belcourt also supervised an out-migration project that sent a few hundred young Acadians to settle in Lower Canada and New Brunswick where there was more tolerance for the French language and customs. Today, many descendants of Island Acadians still live in Quebec and New Brunswick.

Acadian Cultural Nationalism

The emergence of a sense of Acadian nationalism in the Maritimes in the middle of the nineteenth century helped Island Acadians in their struggle to preserve their culture. In 1864, an Acadian college was built in New Brunswick, and a French newspaper, *Le Moniteur Acadien*, was established three years later. Over the next several years, several other French-language newspapers were founded, including *L'Impartial* in Tignish. The Acadian Teachers' Association, a home and school association, and the Saint Thomas Aquinas Society also emerged to promote French-language education on the Island.

Acadian representatives from across the Maritimes gathered at Memramcook, New Brunswick, in 1881 and in Miscouche, Prince Edward Island, in 1884 to discuss their problems and find ways to preserve their culture. Although most of their resolutions met with failure, the conventions decided on a national feast day, a flag, a motto, and an anthem to help spark a renewed sense of cultural pride and identity. The editor of *Le Moniteur Acadien* wrote, "the flag will be our rallying symbol, the motto the emblem of our aspirations, and the song the expression of our attachment to all that is related to religion and to our native land."

Without government assistance, French-speaking teachers, and money, Island Acadians faced an uphill battle to survive. Gilbert Buote, the son of the Island's first Acadian teacher and a staunch defender of Acadian rights, was one of those who led the struggle for Acadian cultural survival. As a teacher, principal, and founder and

The Acadian flag. The Second Acadian Convention in Miscouche adopted the tri-colour flag and the hymn "Ave Maris Stella" as the Acadian national anthem. Stella Maris is the star of the sea and symbolizes the Virgin Mary, the patron saint of the Acadian people.

editor of *L'Impartial*, Buote successfully fought for French-language school texts, helped establish the Acadian Teachers' Association, campaigned for suitable training for Acadian teachers, and reprimanded Acadians who he felt were too timid to stand up for their rights. "If we truly want to improve the language we speak, if we want the French language to attain the rank that it should have in our schools," he wrote, "let us strive to put suitable books in the hands of our children." Buote wrote the first Acadian novel, *Placide, l'homme mystérieux* (1904), in which a young Acadian detective from

TWO ACADIAN FIRSTS

Stanislaus Francis Perry was born in Tignish as Stanislas-François Poirier. He learned English in a Charlottetown school before returning to Tignish to teach. In 1854, Perry became the first Acadian elected to the Island legislature. Nineteen years later, he was appointed the first Acadian Speaker of the House. When Perry was elected to the House of Commons in 1874, he was the first Acadian to have served in both the provincial assembly and the House of Commons.

Aubin-Edmond Arsenault was born in 1870 into a family in Abram's Village that had Island roots back to 1728. He attended Saint Dunstan's College and taught school for two years before returning to school and becoming a prominent lawyer in Summerside. Aubin's father, Joseph-Octave, was a member of the Island assembly and later became the first Island Acadian in the Senate. Aubin Arsenault was also elected as an MLA, and in 1917 he became the first Acadian provincial premier. Four years later, he was appointed to the Supreme Court of Prince Edward Island.

Île Saint-Jean is summoned to New York to track down criminals who have brought the city to a standstill. Acadians, his message was, can attain international respect and recognition. Although some forward strides had been made, the fight for Acadian rights continued well into the twentieth century.

Death and Disease

The living conditions on Prince Edward Island at the turn of the century were often atrocious. The unsanitary conditions caused by open sewers, outdoor toilets, polluted drinking water, inadequate food, and poorly ventilated and overcrowded homes led to frequent outbreaks of diseases and epidemics. The great killers at this time were typhus, typhoid, smallpox, tuberculosis, and diphtheria.

Smallpox was one of the most dreaded diseases. In the first half of the century, the Island's relative isolation and its scattered population limited the number of smallpox cases, and as a result, many people did not bother getting immunized against the disease. The 1871 census revealed that only one-half of the Island's population was inoculated against smallpox. Thus, when the smallpox virus arrived in Charlottetown in November 1885, it caught the city woefully unprepared. During the summer of 1885, Islanders had watched as the disease swept through Montreal, but had done nothing to prepare for a possible epidemic. Then, on November 12, nine cases of smallpox were reported to the Charlottetown city health officer. The epidemic had begun.

In an attempt to prevent the spread of the virus, the area in which the smallpox was found was immediately quarantined, and remained so until each house had been inspected and its inhabitants had been vaccinated. The government converted the empty lunatic asylum into a hospital, closed all schools and churches, banned public meetings, and ordered the Charlottetown superintendent of vaccination to vaccinate all paupers free of charge. A survey of the city's nine doctors revealed that only six physicians had vaccine on hand, and none had any to spare. All mail and trains leaving the capital were fumigated, and the *Daily Patriot* strove to retain its subscribers by vaccinating all employees and fumigating the paper. Despite these precautions, fifty-five citizens died from smallpox during the outbreak.

On November 23, 1885, the provincial government capitulated to popular demand and made vaccination compulsory for everyone. The following year, the government ruled that no one was allowed to attend or teach school without proof of vaccination. Unfortunately, out-of-sight meant out-of-mind and smallpox recurred periodically into the 1920s as many people refused to be vaccinated.

Hospitals

Because hospitals were commonly viewed as places where people went to die rather than be cured, most citizens reacted strongly against their immediate presence. In 1860, Charlottetown's first hospital was built on Mi'kmaq traditional camping ground on the east side of the harbour. When this structure burned to the ground six years later, another building was erected on the city's outskirts. Within several years, this hospital was filthy and had become a public nuisance. Dr. J. T. Jenkins declared that any patients admitted to it would probably die before receiving treatment.

In 1879, Bishop Peter McIntyre of Charlottetown delivered a rousing sermon on the need for medical services for the city's poor. The resulting donations helped finance the conversion of McIntyre's Episcopal residence on Dorchester Street into a hospital. The Charlottetown Hospital, as the institution was named, opened the next year with a staff of five Grey Nuns and three Franciscan Sisters, and accommodations for fourteen patients. Although the hospital granted entry to clergymen and doctors of all religions, the local Protestant community erected the Prince Edward Island Hospital in 1883 to care for their own patients. Both institutions refused to admit patients with dangerous infectious diseases for fear of contagion.

PRINCIPAL CAUSES OF DEATH

The 1901 census listed the major causes of death as:

Tuberculosis:	224
Senile debility:	170
Bronchitis/pneumonia:	142
Cancer:	44
Heart disease:	43
Meningitis:	42
Influenza:	35
Diphtheria/croup:	32
Whooping cough:	30

The Charlottetown Hospital building

OPEN WIDE

During the nineteenth century, dentistry was largely an itinerant profession. Dentists travelled from town to town, offering their services for a limited time. A typical advertisement published in the *Charlottetown Examiner* in 1857 read: "Dr. Shaw, Dentist, Has arrived in town and taken rooms at the Victoria Hotel, where he will remain for a limited period. Those wishing his services are requested to give him an early call. Ladies waited on at their residence if required."

For the greater part of the nineteenth century, most dental work consisted mainly of tooth extraction and the alleviation of pain. By the end of the century, however, the adoption of ether for general anesthetics and materials such as silver amalgam and gold foil allowed dentists to fill cavities and restore diseased teeth. Dentists also provided collections of artificial teeth. In 1890, for example, J. A. Stackhouse offered the "best sets of teeth, Canadian, American, or English-made, mounted on red, black, or maroon vulcanite rubber bases for $8.00." Since most dentists' offices lacked electricity, patients sat facing the window for better visibility.

Women at Work

Women only made up about ten percent of the work force at the turn of the century. Most working women were young and single, as women were expected to quit their jobs when they married. Most women who worked were employed as teachers, dressmakers, nurses, factory workers, house cleaners, shopkeepers, or secretaries. Since elementary school teaching, dressmaking, and nursing were thought to be part of a mother's natural role, women dominated these occupations and the jobs became thought of as "women's work." No matter what the profession, working women were generally subjected to long hours, strict discipline, and low pay. Even when performing the same job as a male, a woman would earn less. For example, at the turn of the century, the average first-class male teacher earned $440 annually and the average first-class female teacher made $332.

Many Island women were also active in charity work at the turn of the century, establishing, managing, or volunteering for charity organizations and hospital and church auxiliary groups. They raised funds through sales of baked goods, quilts, and other handmade items in order to pay for the maps, globes, chalk, and water buckets that were desperately needed by local schools. Many women also became involved in missionary organizations, for which they organized fundraising drives and served as missionaries in foreign fields. The Women's Baptist Missionary Union of the Maritime Provinces, for example, had twelve Island branches as of 1884.

Public Education

In 1852, the Island became the first Maritime colony to abolish school tuition fees, pay teachers' salaries, and regulate provincial schooling. Each of the 475 school districts on the Island was entitled to a one-room school, usually offering grades one through ten. Within two years of the legislation, the number of Island students enrolled in schools doubled.

However, the provincial government had yet to decide on what to do about religion in Island schools, and this question plagued the provincial government for the next twenty-five years. The controversy

A typical schoolhouse. Along with the church and the general store, the school was at the centre of each community.

focused on whether the Bible should be authorized for use in public schools. The government finally came to a decision in 1877, and decreed that all public schools be non-sectarian. Teachers were permitted to open school with Scripture readings (without comments), and student attendance was optional. As well, some urban schools were allowed to be Protestant or Catholic.

Island teachers were the poorest paid in Canada and averaged less than four years on the job in the late nineteenth century. As a result, it wasn't unusual for students to have as many as three teachers in a year. The high turnover rate of teachers meant that Island schools were often forced to hire unqualified teachers, or if no one could be found, leave the schools vacant.

In 1898, the Island government made school attendance compulsory for eight- to thirteen-year-olds, but this rule was seldom enforced. School attendance averaged only sixty-two percent, and it was even lower for children in the older grades, who were often needed to help on the farm. As a result, fourteen percent of the population at the turn of the century could not read and write and nine percent could not read.

RULES FOR TEACHERS, 1879

The following list of rules governing teachers' behaviour and morality indicates the low status of educators and the prevailing values of society:

1. Teachers each day will fill lamps and clean chimneys before starting work.

2. Each teacher will bring a bucket of coal and a scuttle of coal for the day's sessions.

3. Mark your pens carefully. You may whittle nibs to the individual taste of the children.

4. Men teachers may take one evening a week for courting purposes or two evenings to attend church regularly.

5. After ten hours of school, you may spend the remaining time reading the Bible or other good books.

6. Women who marry or engage in unseemly conduct will be dismissed.

7. Each teacher should lay aside, from each pay a goodly sum for his benefit during their declining years so that they will not become a burden to society.

8. Any teacher who smokes, uses liquor in any form, frequents pool or public halls, or gets shaved in a barber shop, will give good reason to suspect his worth, intention, integrity and honesty.

CHAPTER ELEVEN
The Empire at War

In 1900, Britain's Queen Victoria presided over an empire that included nearly twenty percent of the earth's surface and twenty-five percent of the population. Joseph Chamberlain, the British minister in charge of the colonies, sought to bring the British Empire closer together as one economic, political, and military unit to further strengthen British power. His best opportunity arose in October 1899, with the onset of the Boer War.

During the Napoleonic Wars in the early nineteenth century, Britain had captured the Dutch colony at the southern tip of Africa in order to secure the ocean route to India. Unhappy with British rule, the descendants of the early Dutch colonists, the Boers, trekked into the interior of the colony and established their own republics, the Orange Free State and Transvaal. With the discovery of diamonds in the Orange Free State in 1869 and the world's largest gold field in the Transvaal in the 1880s, tensions grew

This Canadian postage stamp illustrates the extent of the British Empire in 1898.

between the Boers and the English—both of whom wanted to profit from the discoveries. As a result, the Boer War began in the fall of 1899.

When Great Britain asked Canada for military help in defeating the Boers, Prime Minister Wilfrid Laurier's first response was to refuse. He believed that Canada had no reason to fight the Boers, for whom many French Canadians felt some empathy because they had also been defeated and colonized by Britain. English Canadians, on the other hand, wanted closer ties to the British Empire and demanded that Laurier send Canadian troops to South Africa. As a compromise, Laurier promised to pay for the recruitment and transport of a battalion of Canadian volunteers to South Africa, but made it clear that once they arrived, they would be the responsibility of Great Britain.

The Boer War marked the first occasion in history that large contingents of Canadian troops served abroad. In November 1899, the first Canadian contingent, which consisted of one thousand men—including thirty-two Islanders—set sail for South Africa.

The first Canadian blood of the Boer War was spilled in February 1900 at the Battle of Paardeburg. This nine-day battle was viewed as a major Boer defeat and a great national triumph for Canada, whose troops distinguished themselves in battle. Canadians also participated in numerous other battles. Although the Canadian soldiers were poorly trained, one British commander commented that while "Canada's soldiers...lack to some extent the barrack yard polish...they more than make up for it in spirit and dash and a certain air of self-reliant readiness to hold their own."

Over the three years of the war, 7,368 Canadian volunteers—including 125 Islanders and 12 female nurses—served in South Africa. When the war ended in May 1902, it had cost Canada almost $3 million and 277 lives.

The war temporarily distracted Islanders from their economic woes. So popular was the idea of serving the empire, or escaping unemployment at home, that Islanders surpassed all other provinces in their enthusiasm to enlist. The Islanders that remained home

---

THE FIRST TIME I SAW MAMA CRY

Years after the first Canadian contingent left for South Africa, Islander William Riggs recalled his brother Alfred's departure:

The morning he left to march with his company to the station was the first time I ever saw Mama cry. She felt that she could not bear to see the train leave with her boy on it, so she kissed him goodbye in the doorway. The rest of us walked to the station. Flags flying, people cheering, smiles, tears and the band playing 'The Girl I Left Behind Me' made an impression that has stayed with me all these years.

Just before the train pulled out, Mama ran into the station. She had run at least ten blocks, because she had to see him just once more. He did not see her at first, and we yelled as loud as we could, 'Alf, Alf, here's Mama!'... and he smiled at her as long as he could see her, as the train moved slowly out of the station."

Less than four months after his departure, Alfred Riggs was killed in the war.

Canadian troops in Bloemfontein, South Africa, 1900

followed the course of the war through the newspapers and poured into the streets to celebrate every major British victory, closing the stores and schools and sounding the horns of ships in the harbour. Lucy Maud Montgomery confided to her diary, "There is something stirring and exciting and tingling about it all even here in this quiet little Island thousands of miles from the seat of war. Everyone is intensely interested in the news."

The War to End All Wars

When Great Britain declared war on Germany on August 4, 1914, Canadian Prime Minister Robert Borden and his wife, Laura, were golfing in Muskoka, Ontario. Borden rushed to Ottawa by train, but declared that he did not think that the fighting would amount to very much. That evening, Charlottetown's fire bell sounded to announce the beginning of what became known as the "War to End All Wars." The next day, the headline on the front page of the *Guardian* declared, "THE DIE IS CAST."

As a member of the British Empire, Canada was automatically at war when Great Britain was at war. However, as with the Boer War, Canada could decide for itself how much to participate. Canadians were united in their determination to aid Britain and defeat the axis powers of Germany, Italy, and Austria-Hungary. Imbued from youth with sentiments of loyalty to the "mother country," thousands of Canadians flocked to enlist to serve God and country. Some enlisted for the excitement, glory, and medals that they hoped would be theirs. Others joined for free room and board and $1 a day. Few people expected the war to last past Christmas.

Initially, Canada's armed forces consisted of an army of thirty-one hundred men, a militia of some sixty thousand, and a navy of one light and one heavy cruiser. Within a few weeks of the declaration of war, however, tens of thousands of young men had gathered at the Valcartier Camp near Quebec City for training. On October 1, 1914, the first division of Canadian troops, accompanied by Newfoundland soldiers, sailed to Great Britain to complete its training. It was the largest convoy ever to cross the Atlantic.

ISLAND NURSE EXTRAORDINAIRE: GEORGINA FANE POPE

Four nurses and one medical officer accompanied the first Canadian contingent to the Boer War. The Canadian Army Nursing Services in South Africa was led by Georgina Fane Pope, a native of Charlottetown and daughter of William Henry Pope, an Island Father of Confederation. In 1903, Pope was awarded the Royal Red Cross by Queen Victoria for conspicuous service in the field. She was the first Canadian to receive the award.

In 1917, at age fifty-five, Pope served in France in the First World War. Shell shock, overwork, and constant air raids played on her nerves, and after eight months at the front, she was invalided home. When Georgina Fane Pope died in Charlottetown in 1938, veterans of both the Boer and the First World War attended her military funeral.

Georgina Fane Pope, circa 1890

Thanks to enthusiastic enlistments, the Canadian army swelled to 250,000 by 1915. Early in February 1915, the 1st Canadian Division reached France and was introduced to trench warfare. Faced with the realities of dirt, disease, and death, their illusions of military glory quickly disappeared. After the initial German advances, the battle on the Western Front quickly turned into a stalemate. Both sides dug in opposite each other in three or more parallel lines of trenches that zigzagged for nearly a thousand kilometres from Belgium to Switzerland. Their defence systems consisted of thousands of kilometres of trenches, tunnels, deep underground shelters, minefields, barbed wire, and machine guns. Soldiers faced their enemies across a narrow strip of territory called "No Man's Land" that was protected by enemy machine gun fire, artillery, and snipers.

Prior to an attack, artillery pounded the front lines to soften up the enemy and destroy the barbed wire the soldiers would otherwise have to cut through. Then, in the face of withering machine gun fire, the men went "over the top." When their guns jammed, the soldiers used bayonets for killing. For most soldiers, the war consisted of the stench of rotting bodies; the noises of whistling shells and the staccato rattle of machine guns; knee-high mud; and constant moans from the wounded. Mt. Albion's Spurgeon Jenkins recalled the Second Battle of Ypres: "Above the screams of the shells you could hear the groans of the dying. It was enough to turn a man's hair gray, and I sincerely hope I will never pass through the like again."

The soldiers fought, ate, slept, and died in the trenches. Permanently damp at the best of times, with Europe experiencing one of its wettest periods in history, the persistent rain turned the trenches into rivers. Often cold and wet, the soldiers endured intermittent sleep, poor sanitation, cold food, frostbite, trench foot, and the ever-present threat of death from shell fire, gas, bullets, and bayonets.

Canadian soldiers distinguished themselves in battle. They endured the first poison gas attack at Ypres, the mud at Passchendaele, and the battles of the Somme, Vimy Ridge, Amiens, Hill 70, and many others. For a nation of eight million people, Canada's war effort was remarkable. Some Island soldiers, such as Harry Leslie, were decorated for bravery, but more suffered Private William Henry Coffin's fate and were buried quietly overseas.

In the early stages of the war, airplanes were used solely for reconnaissance. Soon, advances in technology and military strategy turned them into killing machines. Bombers and fighters destroyed railroad centres and industrial targets far behind enemy lines, hunted submarines at sea, and duelled in the air. Wendell W. Rogers of Alberton wrote the following account to his father of his duel with a German pilot in 1917:

> *I got within 30 yards of him, behind and just under his tail. Let him have 60 rounds, when he burst into flames. The old Hun glided down about 4,000 feet, burning beautifully, and I went after him again, fearing he might be able to put the fire out; but, before I got within striking distance he exploded, and, with the exception of one wing, there was not a piece bigger than my hand touched the ground. This occurred over 'No Man's Land,' so my hopes for that piece of wing as a souvenir were shattered. We have a score to pay back to those blighters for some sleepless nights and their damage to London.*

CANADIANS IN THE WAR

August 4, 1914:	First World War begins
April 1915:	Battle of Ypres
June 1916:	Battle of Mount Sorrel
September 1916:	Battle of the Somme
April 1917:	Battle for Vimy Ridge
August 1917:	Battle for Hill 70
November 1917:	Canadians capture Passchendaele, Belgium
August 1918:	Battle of Amiens
November 11, 1918:	Armistice signed

One-third of all pilots died in combat, including 1,600 of the 25,000 Canadians who served in the British air force. Approximately 50 of these pilots were from Prince Edward Island.

A total of 619,636 men and women served in the Canadian forces during the First World War. Of these, 66,655 gave their lives and another 172,950 were wounded. Prince Edward Island contributed 3,696 soldiers, including 32 of the 64 militarily eligible

Mi'kmaq males on Lennox Island. Approximately 2,500 women, including 62 Island women, served as nursing sisters overseas.

The Home Front

Although Prince Edward Island was not attacked, signs of the war were everywhere. In Summerside, for example, the Crystal Rink was turned into a shooting range, and Happyland Theatre showed military documentaries aimed at boosting morale. Women in nearly every community organized donation drives to gather food, clothes, and other necessities for the soldiers. Church groups and various aid organizations such as the Imperial Order of the Daughters of the Empire, the Women's Patriotic Association, and the Red Cross Society raised funds, knitted socks, made pyjamas and underwear, rolled bandages, sent care packages, and helped recruit men for the armed forces. They also encouraged people to buy "Victory Bonds" to help the government finance the war. Islanders bought $2.9 million of Victory Bonds.

Conscription

As the war dragged on and casualties mounted, groups such as the Prince County Patriotic Recruiting Society scoured the countryside for volunteers, and local newspapers such as the Summerside *Journal* published recruitment ads with declarations such as, "It is better to wear khaki and fight for Britain than to wear shackles and slave for

JACK TURNER: WAR PHOTOGRAPHER

Brenton Harold "Jack" Turner, a soldier from O'Leary, Prince Edward Island, secretly recorded the war on his camera. Although it was illegal for soldiers to carry a camera lest the enemy make use of the pictures or the graphic details dampen the spirits of those at home, Turner hid this two-by-three-inch Kodak camera in his sleeve or under his pillow, and surreptitiously snapped a visual history of the war on the Western Front, including the battles at Ypres, the Somme, and Vimy Ridge.

Since the soldiers' mail was censored, Turner wrote letters home to his fiancée to request "cigarettes," a code word for film, which his fiancée sent to him hidden in fruitcakes. Turner used abandoned cellars to develop his pictures and trusted his friends to keep them safe.

Turner returned to O'Leary after the war, took up farming, and lost interest in photography. However, after winning first prize in a photography contest with one of his old pictures, his interest was rekindled and he took up photography again as a hobby.

A First World War recruiting poster

the Kaiser" and "Be a Man! Get into Khaki."

In the spring of 1917, Prime Minister Borden returned from the front convinced that more soldiers were needed to defeat Germany. He approached Wilfrid Laurier, the leader of the Liberal Party, about forming a coalition government to pass compulsory conscription. After Laurier rejected this offer for fear that he would lose the support of Quebec, which was strongly opposed to being forced to fight in another British imperialistic war, Borden called an election for December 17, 1917. The issue was simple—conscription or not.

The conscription issue aroused bitter feelings. Quebeckers objected to being forced to fight in another British war that did not concern Canada, which led to bloody riots. The Laurier Liberals captured 62 of the 65 seats in Quebec, but only 20 constituencies outside Quebec, including two of the four Prince Edward Island ridings. Borden captured 153 seats. The conscriptionists had won, but in the process, Canada had been divided along French-English lines. Ultimately, 120,000 men were conscripted, but when the war ended earlier than expected on November 18, 1918, less than one-quarter of them had actually seen action.

Returning Home

After four years of fighting, the returning soldiers met with large cheering crowds as they arrived at ports and train stations across the country. Much had changed since they had left for the war. Prices had universally skyrocketed, causing worries about inflation; automobiles were common sights; women were allowed to vote in

The victory parade along Water Street in Summerside, 1919

federal elections; alcoholic beverages were more difficult to obtain; and income tax was a way of life for the more wealthy.

Tragically, a new disaster was looming. The Spanish flu swept into Canada aboard troopships in September 1918. By October, Charlottetown had more than six hundred influenza patients. Soldiers who had seen their comrades die in battle came home to find their families wiped out. The Spanish influenza killed more than twenty million people around the world and claimed as many Canadian lives as had the war.

The epidemic was spread by germs broadcast by coughing, sneezing, or talking. Infected people either recovered within two or three days, or died of such complications as meningitis and pneumonia. In order to prevent the spread of the virus, provincial health officials closed schools, theatres, and churches; restricted business hours; cancelled sporting events; banned public funerals; and ordered that the dead be buried within twenty-four hours. Hospitals sterilized telephone mouthpieces and courts repealed the rule that required witnesses to kiss the Bible. Everywhere, church bells chimed sombrely for the mounting dead. Some people wore masks, stopped kissing, doused themselves with alcohol, tied salt herring around their necks, or sprinkled sulphur on their shoes to ward off germs. St. Dunstan's

College turned one of its buildings into a hospital to treat the growing number of patients.

Women Win the Right to Vote

The First World War was the catalyst that persuaded Canadian politicians to give women the vote. By working in factories, looking after the farms, raising money, and a hundred other ways, women had shown their capability of handling what was traditionally thought of as man's work, and it seemed appropriate that they be entrusted with the right to vote.

In 1910, Lucy Maud Montgomery informed a reporter, "I would have no use for suffrage myself. I have no aspirations to be a politician. I believe a woman's place is in the home." Five years later, however, as with many women, the war had changed her view and Montgomery told another reporter, "I do hope that it will in some measure open the eyes of humanity to the truth that the women who bear and train the nation's sons should have some voice in the political issues that may send those sons to die on the battlefields."

More importantly, Prime Minister Borden needed to win the 1917 election to introduce conscription, and he realized that extending the vote to women could help him achieve this feat. Borden introduced the Wartimes Elections Act in 1917 and gave the vote to the wives, mothers, and sisters of soldiers, as well as to women serving in the armed forces—individuals who he expected would vote for conscription.

"YOU SHOULD BE ASHAMED OF YOURSELF"

Elsie Inman described the problems some women had when it came to voting:

Most of the women were afraid of their husbands. The majority of husbands refused to let them vote. Well, I remember taking a woman -- she said she'd vote, but she was scared to vote because her husband threatened her if he saw her at a poll. She was anxious to vote and I said, "would he know you if you were dressed up in other clothes?" Well, she didn't think he would, so I went home and she was about my size. We wore veils in those days, so I took my clothes and coat and put the veil on her and took her to vote....

I went to the door to get another woman to vote and her husband met me and said, "Get out of this, trying to lead my wife astray, you should be ashamed of this. You're from a nice family, and have a good husband, you should be ashamed of yourself."

The following year, all women except Aboriginals and Asians were enfranchised and allowed to run for federal office.

Provincially, the Island trailed all provinces but Quebec in granting women the vote. In 1916, Margaret Rogers Stewart and Elsie Inman formed the Women's Liberal Club of Prince Edward Island and set out to convert men to their views supporting the enfranchisement of women. As the following patronizing editorial from a 1921 issue of the Charlottetown *Examiner* indicates, they faced a difficult task: "Can women perform aright the multifarious duties of the home, follow the fashions closely, give time to social matters, take a lively interest in current news and gossip, etc., and also attend closely to matters and questions of political importance?" The Women's Liberal Club knew they could, and began lobbying members of the legislature.

Finally, in 1922, thanks in part to the efforts of the Women's Liberal Club, Island women received the franchise. Premier John Bell justified the provincial government's decision to give women the vote by arguing that they now voted in federal elections, had helped win the war, and that it would broaden their "subjects of conversation and study," and also noted that the public would benefit from their advice on matters of morals, health, and the family.

CHAPTER TWELVE
The Interwar Years: Good Times, Hard Times

The interwar years brought many changes to the Island. In the 1920s, modern ideas and technology ushered in a new era—women began to make inroads in traditionally male activities, the Red Cross created a public health system, and the rise of the automobile revolutionized the Island way of life and spurred local industry. But the Depression of the 1930s soon brought poverty to many Island families, as agriculture and fish prices dropped and the cost of farm machinery and manufactured goods increased, making it nearly impossible for Islanders to turn a profit.

Rural Life in the Interwar Years
Modern amenities were slow to take hold in the rural areas of the Island during the interwar years. Outside the larger centres, Islanders managed without electricity, or received it only for a few hours in the evening. This usually meant carrying water into the house for sponge baths in galvanized tubs, ironing clothes with heavy metal irons heated on wood stoves, using outdoor toilets, cleaning clothes with washboards and hand-operated wringers, using large blocks of ice to keep food chilled, operating battery-powered radios, and dealing with the absence of electric lights and central heating. Islander Jean Halliday MacKay recalled, "We were the first family in the community to put a bathroom in the house, probably either just before or after 1918 when Mother and Dad were married. One horrified man is reported to have said, 'They are going to shit in the house!'"

Country stores were natural gathering places for news and gossip. To supplement the limited variety of goods offered at local stores, Island farmers relied on mail-order catalogues from Eaton's, Simpsons, or Holman's. When these catalogues became outdated, the farmers

Students at the Charlottetown Business College, circa 1920s. The hair and dress styles were typical of this era.

recycled them as hockey shin pads, fuel for the fire, or toilet paper for the outhouse.

The High Life

In urban areas throughout North America, the years after the First World War were a time of intense change. Traditional values were being cast aside, new technological advances were being embraced, new forms of art and architecture were emerging, and the stock market was soaring. This era—known as the "Roaring Twenties" or the "Jazz Age"—is typified by flappers with short skirts and bare legs, the Charleston, jazz, rum-running, Ford Model T's, and radios. As a predominantly rural province, most Islanders outside Charlottetown or Summerside did not have the time or the inclination to actively participate in the Jazz Age. However, Island newspapers inundated the province with American popular culture via cartoons, advice columns, fashion articles, sporting activities, and movie and other advertisements.

Women's Higher Education

Although females were admitted to Maritime universities beginning in the 1870s, the Island's only institution of higher learning, St. Dunstan's College, did not accept female students. As a result, Island women had to go elsewhere if they wanted to obtain post-secondary education.

During the 1930s, the Sisters of St. Martha requested that several of their members be allowed to attend classes at St. Dunstan's. The order had been asked to teach grades 11 and 12 at the district high school in Kinkora, but at this time the government required all high school teachers to have a university degree. Since the order could not afford to send its prospective teachers to a mainland university, Sister Mary Paula, the congregation's mother general, lobbied St. Dunstan's to make an exception to their rule against admitting women. The university acquiesced, and in 1939, Sister Mary Peter (Bernice Cullen) and Sister Ida Mary (Mary Jeanette Coady) became the first women to attend St. Dunstan's.

However, the two women were not always treated equally at the university. One of Sister Mary Peter's professors requested that she not attend the classes on ethics and marriage, but failed to inform her when she could resume classes. As well, even though Sister Mary Peter earned the highest marks of all graduating students in 1941 and should have been awarded the Governor General's medal for her achievement, the university changed the rules and awarded the medal to a male student.

The sisters' excellent academic performance no doubt made it easier for

CO-ED DAYS ARE HERE AT LAST

In 1942, the female students at St. Dunstan's wrote the following poem for the university's newspaper, the *Red and White*, announcing that they were there to stay:

During the summer, one bright day,
All the people were heard to say,
A dreadful thing has come to pass,
Three girls are entering the Freshmen Class.
Two girls are taking junior, too,
Now what on earth will the fellows do?
They'll have to wash behind their ears,
Because the dirt might shock the "dears,"
They'll have to dress real nice, and shave,
And in their hair they'll press a wave, ...
Who can they be? What are their names?
I'd like to meet these Co-ed dames. ...
Please welcome us into your class,
For Co-ed days are here at last.

the college to accept additional women. The Second World War also played a role in relaxing gender restrictions. In 1944, Gertrude Butler became the first laywoman to graduate from St. Dunstan's, and by the early 1950s almost ten percent of the students were women.

Prohibition

In 1918, the federal government prohibited the import, manufacture, and sale of alcoholic beverages in Canada. However, during the 1920s, every province except Prince Edward Island abandoned Prohibition in favour of government-operated liquor stores. Not until 1948 could Islanders purchase a legal alcoholic beverage.

There was a loophole in the Island's Prohibition rules—"medicinal alcohol" was allowed as long as it was prescribed by a doctor, and prescriptions for alcohol could be filled at a local drug store. As a result, Islanders flocked to their doctors, complaining of all different sorts of ailments that warranted a prescription for alcohol. In a nine-month period from 1919 to 1920, for example, Island doctors issued 34,200 prescriptions for medicinal alcohol. "Epidemics" and long line-ups invariably occurred during the Christmas season. In response, the government restricted doctors to a monthly quota of fifty prescriptions.

Along with medicinal alcohol, drinking moonshine and illegal bars and speakeasies were popular among certain sectors of society. Between 1922 and 1930, for example, the Island police conducted more than six thousand raids of speakeasies, which resulted in more than one thousand convictions and the confiscation of copious amounts of illegal alcohol. One raid in Rustico in 1923 produced eleven hundred gallons of rum and fourteen cases of whisky.

Between 1919 and 1933 the United States banned the sale, but not the consumption, of alcohol. Since Canadian laws did not prevent the exportation of liquor across international or provincial borders, the spirits trade to the United States provided an alternative source of income for the depressed fishing industry. Hundreds of Maritime fishing vessels were refitted and used to quench American thirst during the era of American Prohibition.

Some ships smuggled liquor from the French islands of St. Pierre and Miquelon into Prince Edward Island. These so-called rum-runners lured government patrols away and then landed their illegal cargo in one of the Island's many deserted bays or coves. Other tactics they used to smuggle the alcohol in involved hiding liquor in lobster traps or attaching it to buoys.

In 1930, the province created its own police force to combat this trade. This small contingent in khaki and navy blue uniforms patrolled rural areas; enforced the Lord's Day Act, which required observance of the Sabbath; policed automobile traffic; and deported vagrants to New Brunswick, but were generally unsuccessful in enforcing the unpopular liquor laws. In 1932, the Royal Canadian Mounted Police replaced the provincial police force. The Mounties proved no more effective than the provincial police in controlling the liquor trade, however, and rum-running did not end until the Island government rescinded Prohibition in 1948 in favour of government-operated liquor stores.

The end of Prohibition did not mean an end to strict government regulations, however, as the Island adopted a system of permits and quotas to restrict alcohol consumption. According to the new rules, individuals could make maximum weekly purchases of one case of beer or twenty-four ounces of spirits, or a combination of the two. Tourists had to pay twenty-five cents for a similar privilege. Although these restrictions were abolished in 1960, taverns and bars remained forbidden until the mid-1960s, and out-of-the-home alcohol consumption was limited to legions and licensed non-profit clubs. As late as 1970, the Island had only twenty or so licensed restaurants and a dozen lounges, and advertisements for alcohol were forbidden.

Mona Wilson and Public Health

Mona Wilson was undoubtedly the most important individual in the development of public health in Prince Edward Island. In 1923, after working for the American Red Cross in Siberia and the Balkans, Wilson accepted an offer to become the chief Red Cross public health nurse in Prince Edward Island. Following her meeting with the Red

Cross board of directors, Wilson "felt like weeping" when she discovered how wide-ranging her responsibilities were. In the absence of a provincial health department, Mona Wilson and her small staff were responsible for initiating medical inspections in the schools; establishing dental clinics, Junior Red Cross clubs, tuberculosis chest clinics, and crippled children's camps; and organizing province-wide smallpox and diphtheria vaccinations. Wilson was also responsible for staffing a health clinic in Charlottetown and talking to various women's groups about the necessity of planting vegetable gardens, drinking milk, and eating wholesome food.

A week after her meeting with the board of directors, Wilson and her assistant left Charlottetown by train to inspect the rural schools. From the railway stations they travelled by horse and buggy. They had difficulties finding the small rural schools, which were not marked on any map. "We would stop on the top of a hill and scan the countryside for a pair of outside toilets," Mona later recalled, "and that would be the indication of a school!"

Wilson was amazed at the large number of Island children who had diseased tonsils and adenoids, impetigo, ringworm, and head lice. Approximately ninety-six percent of the students suffered from at least one of these problems. More distressing was the

TOOTH PROBLEMS

The public did not become aware of the terrible state of Island children's teeth until the Canadian Red Cross Society conducted medical inspections of the province's schools in the early 1920s. The Red Cross nurses were shocked at the high proportion of Island children who had decayed teeth. In some homes there was only one family toothbrush, and it was used only on Sundays and holidays. "From my experiences," Mona Wilson informed a class of prospective teachers in 1929, "there are many who seem to think it quite unnecessary to save teeth by having them filled, that the thing to do is to wait until they ache then go to the dentist and have them pulled.... They will shrug their shoulders and say 'oh well, Mary will have to get false teeth.'" As a result, persuading families to get regular dental check-ups was an uphill battle.

One of the factors contributing to the Islanders' poor dental health was the lack of dentists in the province. The Island only had one dentist for every 4,660 people in 1923—only Quebec had a worse dentist-to-population ratio. Furthermore, all twenty-two Island dentists lived in Charlottetown and Summerside, making it difficult for rural Islanders to get treatment. Improvements in dental health would not come until after the Second World War.

large number of pupils who were underweight for their height and showed signs of malnutrition.

Wilson and the Red Cross nurses attempted to solve these health problems by organizing health clinics, conducting vaccination drives, visiting schools, and talking with parents. The nurses' emphasis on drinking milk, eating whole wheat, having cleaner homes, installing ice boxes and screen doors, and planting vegetable gardens helped promote fuller and richer lives. As a result of the nurses' efforts, from the moment of birth, every Island child stood a better chance of surviving than was previously the case.

The Rise of the Automobile
The war smoothed the path for automobiles on Prince Edward Island. In 1913, the provincial government had repealed its ban on automobiles and allowed their use on Mondays, Wednesdays, and Thursdays, but only on certain roads. Each community now had the right to decide whether it would permit automobiles. The result of these new rules was instant confusion. If a car broke down on Thursday, its owner had to wait until Monday before driving home. If an automobile owner lived in an area that prohibited cars, he or she had to pull the car by horse to an area that allowed them. To add to the confusion, some farmers blockaded roads to prevent automobiles from frightening their horses.

When this restrictive automobile legislation was removed in 1918, the era of the automobile began. Children amused themselves by writing down the licence numbers of cars that went by and hurried home to look in car registration books to see where the drivers lived. Lucy Maud Montgomery had mixed feelings about the automobile coming to the Island. "In one way I'm rather pleased," she wrote, "I hate to hear the Island made fun of for its prejudice against cars. On the other hand I resent their presence, I wanted to think that there was one place in the world where the strident honk-honk of a car-horn could never jar on the scented air."

By the 1920s, an automobile was becoming a necessity for Islanders. Cars revolutionized society. They enabled farmers to come to town

Water Street in Summerside lined with cars, circa 1938

to shop and sell their goods and friends and relatives to visit one another on a more regular basis. They affected the layout of cities, prompted the building of roadside motels and restaurants, and spurred the establishment of new industries—every town had an automobile dealership, gas station, and repair shop. American tourists, most of whom came by car, added millions to the local economy.

Despite the initial resistance to automobiles among Islanders, cars quickly grew in popularity. In 1921, for example, the Island had one car for every fifty-three people, compared with the national average of one per twenty-eight people. By 1931, however, the Island had narrowed the gap to one car for every thirteen people, compared to the national average of one for every ten people.

Early cars were an adventure. Most automobiles had no heater and had to be hand-cranked to start. Flat tires were a common occurrence. To repair a flat tire, motorists had to take off the tire, remove the inner tube, patch it, push it back, and then put the tire back on the wheel. There were no paved roads in the province until the 1930s, and the red clay roads were easy to slide off of on rainy days. "One expected to spend at least part of each bad day in the ditch," Mona Wilson explained to her sister. Without anti-freeze, many drivers jacked their cars onto wooden blocks and left them there for the winter.

Engineering advances gradually made driving more practical and enjoyable. Adjustable seats were patented in 1920. The next year, stoplights were added, and in 1923, balloon tires, which provided a smoother ride, were adopted. Soon after, the addition of brake lights and a foot pedal, which replaced the accelerator button, increased vehicle safety.

Making a Living
In the 1920s, the Island economy continued to be based mainly on agriculture, fishing, and silver fox farming. With no large industries or forest and mineral wealth to tax, the Island relied heavily on federal subsidies to maintain its standard of living. Similar to the other Maritime provinces, the Island felt alienated from the rest of the country, which was prospering. The decline in demand for fish and coal put added strains on the economy of the region. Already, many large Island companies had moved to Central Canada. Railway freight rates, which had doubled since the end of the war, made it too expensive to ship goods to Central Canada. Tariffs favoured the growth of manufacturing companies in Central Canada. The resulting unemployment forced thousands of young people to leave the region.

The fishing industry went into deep decline in the early twentieth century, plagued by poor markets, low prices, increasing competition, and decreasing supplies of some species. In 1915, a mysterious disease crippled the oyster industry, and despite federal regulations that limited fishers from harvesting oysters less than three inches long, it was several decades before the oyster population recovered. Competition from Japan's crabmeat industry and the beginning of an off-Island live lobster business in the United States resulted in a steady decline in the value of canned lobster exports. The success of Tignish Fisheries in shipping live lobsters to the United States in 1927 helped to offset this decline, but the Great Depression shrunk lobster exports to their lowest point in 1933.

Innovations in technology, such as the gasoline engine, also affected the fishing industry. The first motorboats came into use in Prince Edward Island around 1910. They were faster and more manoeuvrable

Children gathering potatoes, circa 1921. According to the 1921 census, one-third of the population was employed in agriculture. Children under ten were frequently employed on their families' vegetable and fruit farms.

than sailing ships, and allowed fishers to fish at greater distances from the shore without the same concern for weather conditions. Gas engines allowed lobster fishers to haul more traps and travel farther from shore. As a result, a little more than a decade after gas engines first came into use, the working sailboat became obsolete. Since distance from a cannery was now not as important for lobster fishers, the lobster cannery industry underwent an amalgamation that saw the number of canneries decline from 250 in 1900 to 103 in 1928, reducing costs but adding to unemployment.

Agriculture, which constituted over eighty percent of the Island's economy in the 1920s, was more prosperous than the fishing industry in the interwar years. Improved fertilizers and the establishment of a government seed potato certification program in 1916 gained the Island a reputation as an area free of crop diseases, and transformed it into Canada's major seed potato region. It was at this time that the popular Irish Cobbler and the Green Mountain varieties of potatoes were introduced. The dairy industry shifted its emphasis from cheese to butter production in the 1920s.

A truck piled high with fox biscuits, 1936

Silver fox pelts, which were now popular as decorative collars and capes, provided additional income and employment during the interwar years. The number of silver fox farms stood at more than seven hundred in 1929 and accounted for about seventeen percent of total agricultural production. Many farmers earned money by selling breeding foxes to off-Island farms. The silver fox industry was so important to the economy of Alberton that a silver fox is depicted on the town's logo. Summerside was the financial capital of the international fur trade. The industry began to wane in the 1930s, but it remained profitable until the 1940s when changing fashions, the increasing popularity of mink and muskrat furs, competition from Scandinavia, and over-production reduced the demand for silver fox pelts.

The Great Depression

In October 1929, the bottom dropped out of the stock market. The Great Depression had begun. The stock market crash affected the whole world. Workers were laid off, causing them to search desperately for jobs that did not exist. The Prairies suffered a five-year drought. Life was bleak everywhere.

The Maritimes was particularly hard hit. Although the Island did not experience the perils of drought and grasshoppers that destroyed Western Canadian crops, the precipitous decline in farm produce and fish prices on the Island brought ruin to many families. The cost of eggs fell from $0.30 a dozen to just $0.08 cents; silver fox pelts dropped from $100 to $28 each; pork declined from $0.16 to $0.03 a pound; and potatoes, which suffered from a British embargo on Canadian potatoes for fear of contamination from the Colorado beetle, sank from $1.50 to $0.06 per 100 pounds. As a result, agricultural income on the Island decreased from $9.8 million in 1927 to $2.3 million five years later.

Prince Edward Island's $146 average income per person in 1932 was the lowest in the country and one-half the Canadian average. Letters written by Islanders to Prime Minister R. B. Bennett during the Depression requested financial aid and described animals slowly starving to death in their stalls, children suffering from malnutrition, and twenty percent of the labour force unemployed. Although prices for farm produce began to improve in 1936, by this time many farmers had no money left for seeds or fertilizer to rebuild their farms. To make matters worse, the cost of farm machinery and manufactured goods increased at a much faster rate than did agricultural prices, making it nearly impossible for farmers to make a profit.

Many Islanders who had left the province in the 1920s for jobs elsewhere returned after being laid off. The level of destitution on the Island was particularly evident in Charlottetown, where fifteen percent of the people became dependent on charity. Rural families could at least feed themselves from their farms, but urban dwellers did not have this luxury. Neither the provincial government nor the majority of the rural populace had much sympathy for industrial workers, and Prince Edward Island was the only province that had no legislation regarding hours of work, minimum wage, factory inspection for health and safety conditions, workers' compensation, and (along with Ontario) did not recognize workers' rights to collective bargaining. To protect local jobs, the Charlottetown police evicted drifters from the city and ran off mainlanders looking for employment.

After weeks, months, and even years of unemployment, Islanders went into survival mode. Families stopped going to doctors and dentists and driving cars. People wore patched clothes and children went sockless in the summer, saving their socks to use as gloves in the winter. Many children dreaded the morning school bell because it meant that the other children would see how poorly they were dressed. Industrious Islanders turned flour sacks into underwear, and filled the holes in their shoes with cardboard. When their silk stockings wore out, women powdered their legs and drew a black line down the back.

The scramble to catch skunks indicated the seriousness of the situation. Prior to the Depression, a New Annan farm had sought to raise skunks for their pelts, but when the public showed no interest in skunk pelts, the farm had set the animals free. The skunks adapted so well to the Island that the province's skunk population soon grew out of control, and the government offered a fifty-cent bounty per snout to control their swelling numbers. Islanders eagerly sought to catch the skunks to cash in on the government's bounty. Some people bootlegged snouts from the mainland, and one imaginative person manufactured fake snouts from cowhide. Skunk trapping became so popular that after only three years, the government had paid bounties on over fifteen thousand skunk snouts.

FEED ME JUNK FOOD

Many Island families lived on subsistence diets during the Great Depression. Mona Wilson wrote of the conditions she witnessed in her role as a public health nurse:

From early spring to late fall I was in the country continuously, staying in a different farm house each night, eating each day the same staple food of the rural people -- salt pork or salt cod, potatoes and turnips. I drank milk to set an example to the children despite the fact there was frequently visible dirt and manure floating on top, and waved the flies away at the same time. All children drank only tea. The milk was required for the foxes and pigs.

Relief Support

The provincial Conservative Party was one of the first casualties of the Depression. Although the Depression was no one's fault, the

Liberals under Walter Lea swept all thirty seats in the 1935 election—a Canadian first. A new government, however, did not mean a new approach to the Island's economic and social problems. With limited financial resources, the provincial government was reluctant to adopt social welfare policies to support destitute Islanders. However, poverty and unemployment were so widespread that the provincial government was forced to help. In response to the widespread unemployment during the Depression, the Island government initiated public works programs in which unemployed Islanders were hired to build bridges and wharves, pave the Trans-Canada Highway, and remodel public buildings, among other things. In Summerside, for example, unemployed workers were hired to construct a seawall and a municipal airport, pave the streets, and improve the water and sewage systems. As a result of such activities, the number of civil servants increased dramatically. In 1933, the province bowed to public pressure and began paying old-age pensions to those seventy years of age or over. It set the maximum pension at fifteen dollars, established a strict means test, and made it mandatory for children to support their parents.

The Island's various churches also offered aid to impoverished members of the community, offering food, clothing, and other forms of assistance. Roman Catholics, who comprised forty-five percent of the Island's population, benefited from the activities of the Sisters of St. Martha, who nursed at the Charlottetown Hospital, taught at the Kinkora high school, and serviced the St. Vincent's Orphanage and the Sacred Heart geriatric facility. The sisters also opened a social services department for the poor—within the first six months of its operation, they had visited 1,250 homes, clothed sixty-two children, cared for ten bedridden patients, helped in nine maternity cases, and attended to six dying people.

Unlike the provincial government and the churches, the federal government was of little help to impoverished Islanders. Because federal relief programs matched the amount spent by each province, Prince Edward Island received less money per capita than the wealthier provinces—Island relief recipients received an average of

$1.93 a month in 1935, compared to $6.18 for those receiving federal relief payments outside the region.

Working Together: Co-operatives

When American professor John T. Croteau drove into North Rustico in 1933, he found it "a picture of misery and despair." The residents' incomes were below subsistence level and many families "existed on one or two scanty meals a day" in the winter. When he returned twelve years later, he found a prosperous community—thanks to the activities of the resident pastor, who had organized study clubs and helped establish a credit union, a fishers' union, and a co-operative lobster factory.

Co-operative ventures such as these multiplied significantly during the Depression. Dr. Moses Coady of St. Francis Xavier University provided the spark behind the rapid growth of co-operatives. Coady was the founder of the Antigonish Movement, which sought to make common people self-sufficient. Working with St. Dunstan's University, Coady formed study groups throughout the province to examine the major economic problems of the day, raise money for self-help projects, and provide entertainment through dances, card games, and other social events.

Copying Coady's methods, Islanders formed credit unions and co-operative stores, and established marketing and warehousing organizations. By 1931, the Co-operative Egg and Poultry Association had thirty-eight hundred members; the Potato Growers' Association was purchasing fertilizers, standardizing grades, eradicating disease, and marketing farmers' crops; and numerous other co-operative ventures were providing a variety of goods and services, including financial loans, food processing,

HELPING OTHERS

The Islanders' philosophy of co-operation and sharing was not limited to their own province. In order to help the drought-stricken Western Canadian farmers feed their families, Islanders sent them sixty boxcars of agricultural produce. This act of generosity, declared one relief official, was "one of the most inspirational gestures in Canadian history. Certainly, if Canadianism means anything, this means a great deal in the shaping of a true and loyal national consciousness."

health care, insurance, telephone service, fertilizer, farm implements, and breeding stock.

Tignish, which established the first fishers' union in Canada in 1924, led the way in the co-operative movement. There, co-operative ventures provided health care, loans, groceries, automobile service, fish processing, and marketing services for Irish Moss, blueberries, and other produce. Although the co-operative movement declined in the 1950s, it remained strong in western Prince County.

Entertainment between the Wars
Despite the hardships of the Great Depression, the 1930s were not without their good times. Many Islanders fondly remember this period for its camaraderie and spirit of co-operation. Islanders did whatever they could to help a neighbour: they left parties held at a poor person's home early so that there would be enough food left over for the rest of the week; organized bees to provide entertainment and help with the haying and ploughing; and shared whatever resources they could afford. Visiting friends and relatives was the most common form of entertainment in the interwar period, and many a winter evening was spent playing card games. Larger groups met at the town hall for concerts, dances, and bingo.

Athletics continued to be popular in the interwar years. Now free from corsets and pounds of underclothing, women were able to play more sports, and Summerside's Crystal Sisters became one of the best women's hockey teams in Canada. Hockey received a major boost in 1930 when the Charlottetown Forum was opened, complete with artificial ice.

Track and field was also popular during this era, and Barney Francis of Lennox Reserve helped the Abegweit Amateur Athletic Association win the Maritime Provinces Track and Field Championships from 1922 to 1924. When Francis won the mile event at the Canadian Track and Field Championships in 1923, he became only the third Islander to hold a Canadian or World Championship.

Another favourite activity for Islanders at this time was going to the cinema. Charlottetown had two movie theatres and Summerside had

The Prince Edward Theatre in Charlottetown, circa 1928

one. Silent movies were rarely silent, and were shown with piano or organ accompaniment, sound effects, and subtitles. The newsreel, a collection of short news clips, became standard, along with cartoons, and perhaps a sports reel or a travelogue.

The first "talkies" on the Island coincided with the onset of the Great Depression. The most popular films on the Island were escapist comedies with famous stars such as Charlie Chaplin and the Marx Brothers. These movies helped distract Islanders from the economic problems and gave them a chance to laugh, if only for a short time. On July 2, 1938, the *Guardian* advertised "talkies" in Canoe Cove on Friday, in Souris on Monday, in Mt. Stewart on Tuesday, and in Montague on Saturday. In areas where there was no electricity, a man came every two weeks or so with a portable projector and a generator, along with pop and chips. In Summerside and Charlottetown, movies usually stayed for two days, unless they were held over. These theatres were air-conditioned and showed first-run movies.

Fantasy, like humour, was a common form of escape. Magazines such as *Maclean's* and *Reader's Digest* published romantic stories that allowed the readers to forget their problems for a short while. Adventure and romance novels also took the readers' minds away from their poverty and unhappiness. Zane Grey's western stories, Ralph Connor's adventure novels, and Lucy Maud Montgomery's Anne of Green Gables series provided Islanders with endless hours of enjoyment during the interwar years.

The advent of the radio in the 1920s provided another form of escapism. The radio made the world seem smaller and provided inexpensive entertainment. Initially, radios were status symbols. A good radio cost as much as a car, although handy individuals could make their own crystal sets for much less. In areas without electricity, radios used storage batteries.

KEITH S. ROGERS: MR. RADIO

Summerside's Colonel Keith S. Rogers was an early radio pioneer. He was fascinated by telegraphy and, at the age of fifteen, built a wireless set in his parents' bathroom. In 1909, Rogers signed on with the Coast Guard as a wireless operator on an icebreaker. Two years later, he built Canada's first successful portable wireless at the Canadian Forces base in Petawawa, Ontario. In 1922, although there were fewer than one hundred Island homes with radio receivers, Rogers began broadcasting noon and evening programs from his living room. To increase his audience, he sold radios.

Keith S. Rogers, circa 1930s

In 1925, the federal government granted Rogers and his friend Walter Burke a commercial license for the broadcasting station CFCY 960 in Charlottetown. In 1936, a more powerful transmitter allowed CFCY to increase its audience throughout the Island and to parts of New Brunswick and Nova Scotia. Three years later, CFCY brought in fiddler Don Messer and his band, *The Islanders*, who became known for their down-east fiddling style. Through its programming, CFCY helped popularize a wide variety of musical styles on the Island, especially country and western.

At the time of his death in 1954, Rogers was planning the first television station on the Island. This project was continued by his son-in-law, R. F. Large. The first television program from Prince Edward Island was broadcast in 1956.

Families crowded around the radio to listen to the latest news, sports, music, drama, or comedy. W. C. Fields, Amos 'n' Andy, and Edgar Bergen kept millions of people on both sides of the border entertained, and no one dared phone a friend while Jack Benny was on. Perhaps the most popular Canadian radio show was *The Happy Gang*. It aired five times a week and featured a cast of musicians who played popular songs peppered with amusing banter, comedy routines, and corny jokes.

Island Tourism

The increasing number of steamships, railways, automobiles, and paved roads in the interwar period made transportation to the Island more reliable and affordable, which led to an increase in tourism. In addition, by the late 1930s provincial and federal governments began to cooperate to promote tourism. Already, the popularity of *Anne of Green Gables*, which attracted thousands of tourists to Cavendish, had shown the economic benefits of tourism. L. M. Montgomery, for example, wrote to a friend in 1928, "You ask in your letter if 'Cavendish has become a place of pilgrimage for my admirers?' Alas, yes. And the chagrin expressed in that alas is not an affectation at all but a genuine regret and annoyance. Cavendish is being over-run and exploited and spoiled by mobs of tourists...."

In 1936, the federal government established the Prince Edward Island National Park of Canada in Greenwich. Three years later, the park was officially opened as part of the seventy-fifth Fathers of Confederation celebrations in Charlottetown. Although this event was couched in terms of promoting national unity, it was primarily an attempt to publicize the Island as a tourist destination. The newly-created Canadian Broadcasting Corporation followed the 1939 celebrations in its first nationwide broadcast. Although the event was a great success, it was soon overshadowed by the start of the Second World War.

CHAPTER THIRTEEN
The Second World War

The First World War destroyed the economies of many European countries. Some people resented the new geographical borders that the victors had created at the end of the war, and distrusted the new democratic forms of government that were created. The Depression intensified these problems. People wanted a way out of the hopelessness, frustration, and insecurity that surrounded their lives. They were ready to follow leaders who promised better things and told them that their problems were somebody else's fault—foreigners, communists, democrats, Jews. In this uncertainty, dictators easily gained control—Benito Mussolini in Italy, Francisco Franco in Spain, and Adolf Hitler in Germany.

Hitler's vision of the "master race" required that Germans everywhere belong to one united Germany. In 1938, the German army swept into Austria and later into Czechoslovakia. On September 1, 1939, German tanks thundered across the Polish border and bombers flattened Warsaw. Two days later, France and Britain declared war against Germany.

TIMETABLE FOR WAR
1933: Hitler comes to power in Germany; Germany begins to rearm
1935: Italy invades Ethiopia
1936: Spanish Civil War begins
1936: Hitler sends German troops into the Rhineland on the French border
1936: Japan, Italy, and Germany sign a treaty of mutual protection
1937: Japan invades China
1938: Germany seizes Austria and then takes Czechoslovakia
September 1, 1939: Germany invades Poland; Soviet Union invades Poland and Finland
September 3, 1939: Great Britain and France declare war on Germany
September 10, 1939: Canada declares war on Germany

To appease French Canadians, who wanted Canada to make its own decisions, the Canadian government under Prime Minister William Lyon Mackenzie King waited one week after Britain and France had joined the war before declaring war on Germany.

A recruitment poster from the Second World War

Canadians again enlisted to fight on foreign soil. This time, the slaughter lasted six long years and killed tens of millions of people.

Nazi armies crushed Poland in less than a month. In the spring of 1940, Denmark fell in one day; Norway in two. The Netherlands was smashed in five days. Belgium took eighteen. Even mighty France was shattered in six weeks. After France fell to Hitler's armies, Italy joined the war on Germany's side. Nearly all of Europe was under German or Italian control by 1941. In December 1941, Japan, which had signed a treaty of mutual protection with Germany and Italy in 1936, attacked American and British positions in the Pacific and swiftly captured Hong Kong (imprisoning several hundred Canadians), the Philippines, Malaya, Singapore, and Sumatra.

In August 1942, in their first major battle, British and Canadian soldiers tasted bitter defeat in Dieppe, France. It wasn't until the following year that Canadian soldiers fought again—this time as part of the invasions of Sicily and Italy. More than 30,000 Canadians were wounded or killed in the liberation of Italy—1,375 were killed just in the battle for the town of Ortona, which became a series of house-to-house fights. The Germans soon developed such a high opinion of the skills and bravery of Canadian soldiers that they put their best troops against them whenever possible. On June 4, 1944, after the fall of Italy, the victorious Canadian and British troops entered Rome.

D-Day, the long-awaited invasion of France, came two days later. Approximately 15,000 Canadian soldiers landed on the beaches in Normandy on D-Day, supported by more than 100 ships and 10,000 sailors from the Royal Canadian Navy. About 340 Canadians were killed and 574 were wounded on this day alone. Two nearby cemeteries contain the bodies of nearly 5,000 Canadians killed during the Normandy campaign. It took eleven months before Western troops met their Soviet allies near the Elbe River in central Germany. Canadians had the task of clearing German forces from the French, Belgian, and Dutch ports during the push towards Berlin. This was slow, dangerous work, as enemy forces fought from behind strong fortifications. In 1945, the Canadian Army played a major role in liberating the Netherlands.

On April 27, 1945, Mussolini was captured and shot by his own people. Three days later, Hitler committed suicide. Germany surrendered on May 8, 1945, and Japan capitulated on August 14, 1945.

Over the course of the war, 1.1 million Canadians served in the armed forces. Prince Edward Island had the highest per capita enlistment rates in Canada, with approximately 9,000 volunteers. Approximately 1,400 Islanders served in the Royal Canadian Navy. Even though Aboriginal Peoples had to relinquish their Indian status, and the government support this status entitled them to, in order to join the war effort, a large number of Island Mi'kmaq volunteered for service during the war. In total, about one-half of all Island males between the ages of 18 and 45 enlisted. More than 460 did not return.

Training Soldiers and Pilots on the Island
In 1939, when William Lyon Mackenzie King agreed to take part in the British Commonwealth Air Training Plan for pilots, Canada's minister of defence, R. L. Ralston, rewarded his constituency of Prince County, Prince Edward Island, with an air training school at St. Eleanors, a bombing and gunnery school in Charlottetown, and aerodromes at Mount Pleasant and Wellington. Later, the government established a secret radar base in Tignish, converted the Charlottetown base into a reconnaissance school, and turned Mount Pleasant into a bombing and gunnery school. These Island schools trained more than twelve thousand pilots over the course of the war and brought immediate prosperity to Prince County by creating a demand for food and services.

A class at the air navigation school in Charlottetown, circa 1944

Air-Raid Sirens and Submarines

Even though the Island was far distant from the war, air-raid drills and blackouts made everyone aware of the dangers. Beginning in January 1942, the threat of invasion from the skies led to a series of practice blackouts. Whistles, horns, or bells announced the beginning of a blackout. During blackouts, all vehicles were required to stop and park for the duration of the alarm; indoor lights were to be shielded from outside view; children were to be kept inside; and phone use was limited. The government erected over forty air-raid sirens in various centres about the Island and built an observation on the roof of the Charlottetown Hotel to catch individuals who broke the blackout rules.

Submarine attacks were another danger to Islanders. In May 1942, a German submarine torpedoed a British steamer near Anticosti Island in the Gulf of St. Lawrence. In September 1942, the HMCS *Charlottetown* was torpedoed, struck a reef, and sank off the Nova Scotia coast. In October of the same year, only seventy kilometres off the Newfoundland coast, a German submarine torpedoed and sank the SS *Caribou*, a railway ferryboat that linked Cape Breton with Newfoundland. These actions caused Islanders to worry that their enemies could sink any ship they wished.

Island Life During the War

The war ended the Depression by stimulating the demand for jobs, food, and materials. By 1941, there were enough jobs for all who wanted them and the farming and fishing industries began to prosper. Lobster and fish prices skyrocketed. Islanders canned hake and mackerel, which were rich in proteins, and sold them to an international company that supplied food to war victims. The loss of the Japanese supply of agar after Pearl Harbor increased the demand for Irish moss as a food additive and gelling product, and as a result, the Island's Irish moss industry grew significantly, providing Islanders with additional jobs and income.

Similar to the First World War, during the Second World War Islanders did whatever they could to support the war effort, giving generously to war-related national campaigns and contributing thousands of pounds of food and clothing. Seventy organizations, including fifty-six Women's Institute branches, made almost eight thousand articles of clothing for the Red Cross in 1943 alone. As well, hundreds of Island women joined the women's divisions of the air force, navy, and army, and approximately seven thousand women left the province to work in war-related plants on the mainland.

Along with the voluntary efforts, the Canadian government instituted a series of mandatory regulations to ensure that as many of the country's resources as possible went to the war effort. In 1942, the federal government sent all Canadians a ration book to limit their purchase of sugar, butter, meat, tea, coffee, and whiskey. The government also limited gasoline for cars to one fill-up a month; regulated clothing styles to reduce the amount of fabric used in frills, cuffs, ruffles, and double-breasted jackets; and required special permits for buying such items as cars, appliances, and rubber tires. The government also encouraged

> **SEX AND THE WAR**
>
> The official Island statistics for 1945 showed that whereas births had declined, the number of children born out of wedlock had increased by thirty-seven percent. There was also a sharp incline in the incidence of venereal diseases, and in 1945 the provincial health officer began to take steps to combat the increase in sexually transmitted diseases.

PROBLEMS IN SUMMERSIDE

Although the Prince County air bases employed a large civilian staff, and were of major economic and social importance to the county, the federal government closed the bases at Wellington, Alberton South, Mount Pleasant, and Tignish at the conclusion of the war, adversely affecting the province's employment situation and the merchants who supplied these bases. Only the St. Eleanors base, which had served as a flying school and later as a reconnaissance school, remained in use after the war. It assumed a vital economic position in the surrounding area, providing local Summerside merchants with a ready market for their goods and civilians with a place of employment.

The staff and instructors at the No. 1 General Reconnaissance School in Summerside, 1944

After the Island successfully resisted two threats in the 1960s and 1970s to close the St. Eleanors base, the federal government finally shut it down in 1989. Since the base had been the second-largest employer on the Island, and had pumped about fifty million dollars into the economy annually, Summerside—the second-largest town in the province—faced difficult economic decisions. With local and provincial assistance, an aircraft manufacturing plant and other businesses moved to the former air base. In response to public pressure over the decision to close the base, the federal government established a goods and services tax (GST) branch in Summerside in 1991. By the time the base closed in 1992, the economic blow had been lessened.

families to plant victory gardens and to save metals, rags, papers, rubber, and glass for the war effort. Children collected string and cigarette and candy wrappers for recycling. The steel that had once made washing machines and automobiles now made bombers.

An Underprivileged Area

Despite the boost the Second World War gave to the Maritime economy, at the end of the war the Maritimes were still the most underprivileged region in Canada. In the years following the war, the average income per person in the Maritimes was about two-thirds of the national average (and fell to less than half for a few years in the 1950s), the region's unemployment rate was more than double the national average, and the region also had the highest rates of illiteracy, infant mortality, and tuberculosis in Canada. In addition, the Maritimes were heavily dependent upon primary sector industries, where employment was often seasonal.

At the urging of Maritime politicians and business people, the federal government took positive measures in the 1950s to reduce regional inequalities within the country. In 1952, the government improved old-age security, which provided money to senior citizens. In 1957, the government initiated an equalization program that transferred money from the richer areas of Canada to poorer provinces such as Prince Edward Island to help improve medical and educational services. It also instituted federal price support payments for farmers to maintain their income levels and unemployment insurance for support in hard times.

Post-War Modernization

During the first two decades after the war the Island began to modernize. Electrification was well under way in the rural areas of the province by the mid-1950s, bringing modern conveniences such as washers and dryers, electric irons, record players, televisions, and toasters. However, improvements were slow in many rural areas, and by 1961 only half of the Island's rural homes had running water, only one-quarter had central heating, and two-thirds lacked indoor plumbing. Seven years later, only thirteen percent of the houses in Tignish had flush toilets, fourteen percent of the homes in North Rustico had a furnace, and fewer than fifty percent of the homes in O'Leary had hot and cold running water.

Paved roads were another sign of progress, and by 1960 the Island had the most paved roads per capita in the country. These roads made school consolidation practical, allowed people to live in the country and commute to the city, and made it possible to become involved in a wide variety of entertainment.

Farmers also began to modernize their operations at this time, bringing in mechanical tools and motorized vehicles to do the work that up until then had been done by horses. Between 1941 and 1961, the use of tractors increased tenfold.

THE BOOB TUBE

Television caught on faster than anyone predicted. In 1952, CBC Television began broadcasting out of Toronto and Montreal. Four years later, CFCY-TV commenced broadcasting from Charlottetown as a CBC affiliate. By 1961, almost seventy percent of Island homes had at least one television set.

At this time, television screens were black and white and viewers had to move the antenna around to receive one of the few available channels or to reduce the "snow" on the screen. When stations signed off for the night, they left a test pattern running to help viewers adjust their contrast, sharpness, and brightness—none of which were automatic.

Television revolutionized life. Magazines advised parents on how best to rearrange their living rooms for optimal viewing pleasure. Families began eating meals in front of the television, and TV dinners were invented. Restaurateurs reported that their establishments emptied prior to popular shows.

CHAPTER FOURTEEN
Contemporary Political and Economic Issues

In the 1970s and 80s, many Islanders began to question the province's direction. Some Islanders pointed to the high unemployment rate and an average income that fell well below the national level to support their demands that Prince Edward Island adopt all the latest technological and economic advances. Other people wished to return to past values, and worried that the Island was losing its separate identity and endangering its environment by adopting non-Island ways. They sought to return Prince Edward Island to its "golden age" in the 1860s, when the people supposedly valued conservation, self-reliance, and community.

By the 1960s, fast-food restaurants such as Dairy Queen, A&W, and Kentucky Fried Chicken had created a strip-mall leading into Charlottetown and Islanders were starting to shop at Eaton's, Zellers, and other mainland-based chains that had established stores on the Island. The Island's first mall, Royalty Mall, opened in 1965, and illustrated the growing movement of people from rural to urban areas. In 1979, lobby groups successfully fought for a temporary ban on the construction of new shopping malls, which they felt were threatening to undermine the traditional country store. They were less successful, however, in their attempt to prevent school consolidation, which they believed would seriously undermine smaller rural communities. This time, the allure of modernization prevailed.

The Question of Land Use
The question of land use also revealed the pull between past values and modernization. In the late 1960s, fears that prime agricultural land was falling under the control of people "from away" awakened old memories of absentee landlords. In 1972, despite free-enterprise

arguments that individuals should be free to dispose of their land to the highest bidder, the Island government passed legislation that required non-residents to gain cabinet approval for land purchases exceeding 10 acres or 330 feet of shorefront property. Four years later, however, non-residents had found a variety of ways to purchase an additional 66,000 acres of Island land, and by 1988 more than 10,000 non-residents owned a total of 140,000 acres of Island land.

Conservative and liberal beliefs also clashed over ownership of agricultural land. In the early 1980s, concerned groups lobbied for legislation to prevent agricultural land from being acquired by large corporations, especially non-Island-owned companies. The government responded in 1982 by limiting corporate landholdings to three thousand acres. However, it set no limit on how many acres a firm could lease.

In 1990, when the provincial government signed agreements with McCain Foods and Cavendish Farms that allowed these two New Brunswick-based companies to build potato-processing plants on the Island, the issue of foreign land ownership re-emerged. The processing plants' supporters revelled in the added revenues the large companies would bring to the Island's economy. The *Guardian* editorialized that year: "This is news almost too good to comprehend.... After decades of shipping mainly raw produce and watching other provinces and countries process and profit from the added value, Prince Edward Island can smile—finally—at future prospects for the industry." However, opponents of the plants warned of the threat the large processing plants posed to small Island farmers who had no bargaining power and questioned the government's commitment to the family farm.

After the plants were built, McCain Foods and Cavendish Farms dominated the agricultural scene, and many people feared that the resulting potato monoculture, driven by the companies' focus on processing potatoes into french fries, was adversely changing the landscape and destroying the natural environment. Poor crop rotation, the destruction of trees and hedgerows, and an over-reliance on spraying were gradually eroding the Island's thin layer of red

PLEASE STAY OFF THE GRASS!

Marram grass on the Island's coast

The botanical name for marram grass means "sand-loving." Marram grass, which is common along Prince Edward Island's coast, is nature's attempt to turn sand into soil that can support life. The grass's roots, which can reach three metres deep in search of water, spread into stringy networks that hold the Island's sand dunes together. Although marram grass is impervious to salt spray, it is not hardy enough to withstand constant human traffic. When humans inadvertently destroy the marram grass along the Island's coastline, the wind carves giant holes in the sand—called blowouts—and turns the once stable dunes into constantly shifting hills unable to support either vegetation or wildlife.

---

topsoil. As the wind carried the precious topsoil away, streams and tidal rivers became clogged with dirt and algae. Heavy rains washed potato pesticides and insecticides into these waters, killing fish and other wildlife, and chemicals leached into the groundwater, which supplied much of the Island's drinking water. Although the introduction of buffer zones between waterways and fields and the reestablishment of hedgerows improved this situation, immediate

An Island potato farm

profit often trumped long-term sustainability, and the environmental problems remained.

Beginning in the 1990s, "green thinking" gradually emerged to challenge the prevailing mood of progress at any cost. The rise in sustainable practices such as reforestation and recycling, and the turn toward cleaner forms of energy such as that derived from windmills, biomass fuels, and wood chips and sawdust, illustrate this change in thinking.

Agriculture

Since the beginning of European settlement, Prince Edward Island has been praised for its agricultural value—variously being termed the "Million Acre Farm" and the "Garden of the Gulf." Although approximately one-half of the province's 1.4 million acres is cleared for farm use, the number of people living on farms has steadily declined since the early twentieth century, from sixty-three percent in 1931 to forty-eight percent in 1951 to less than five percent in 2007. While the number of Island farms has fallen from 10,140 in 1951 to 2,360 in 1991 to 1,700 in 2007, the size of the average farm has increased proportionally, and single-family farms are quickly disappearing.

The Island's signature red topsoil is not very deep, but it is excellent for growing potatoes, which represent the province's most important agricultural commodity. In 2007, for example, potato receipts were $180 million of the total crop of $214 million. Prince Edward Island potatoes accounted for about twenty-five percent of Canada's potato production in 2007–08. Approximately half the Island's potato crop is processed into potato chips and frozen products for the North American market.

Other crops that are popular with Island farmers include soybeans, which are exported to Japan; canola, which is made into oil and used for food and fuel; vegetables such as broccoli, cauliflower, rutabagas, carrots, onions, and Brussels sprouts, which are either processed for off-Island markets or sold to local markets; and fruits such as lowbush blueberries, cranberries, strawberries, raspberries, and apples, which are exported to the United States or sold locally.

In 2006, approximately thirty-five percent of Island farms were devoted to dairy cattle. Similar to other farming industries, dairy production on the Island has become highly specialized and mechanized and chiefly supplies the butter, cheese, and ice cream market.

The Fishing Industry

In 2007, fish and agricultural products comprised two-thirds of the Island's exports. Prince Edward Island's most prominent natural resource is the ocean. Although Islanders harvest herring, cod, hake, salmon, flounder, mackerel, trout, and Irish moss, mollusks and crustaceans comprise

ELMER MACDONALD: DAIRY INNOVATOR

In 1944, at the age of nineteen, Elmer MacDonald began a mixed-farming business in New Glasgow. Later, he moved to Hunter River to concentrate on dairy farming and established the Health Milk Company. MacDonald excelled in creative marketing and by the 1980s he was marketing chocolate milk, cream, and eggnog, as well as four varieties of juice. He also introduced Yo-Go, a blend of yogurt and fruit juices with no artificial ingredients, and effectively marketed it as a natural alternative beverage. In the 1990s, MacDonald successfully launched Elmer's ice cream, yogurt, and frozen yogurt and began appearing in television commercials as "Uncle Elmer." MacDonald gave his products a rustic image to capitalize on the Island's image and appeal to local buyers. In 1996, he sold the company to Farmers' Dairy in Nova Scotia.

Green Gables Heritage Place. The house, part of Prince Edward Island National Park, is famous as the setting of Lucy Maud Montgomery's Anne of Green Gables. *Each year, more than half of the tourists to the Island visit Anne Shirley's home, and Cavendish swells from a population of 267 to 7,000.*

the largest part of the sea harvest. In 2007, for example, they made up more than ninety percent of the value of the sea harvest. Other shellfish commonly harvested by Islanders include scallops and the famous Malpeque oysters.

In recent years, the Maritime fisheries have been particularly hard hit. Over-fishing and low market prices have led to drastically reduced incomes for Maritime fishers. Poaching, foreign vessels operating beyond Canadian control, and growing demand have gradually reduced the stock of fish. To allow time for the fish to replenish themselves, in 1992 the federal government slashed the number of fish that could be harvested and offered income supplements to fishers. So far, the fish stock has remained low. Many Islanders have turned to the scientific culturing of mussels, oysters, salmon, soft-shell clams, and trout, and aquaculture has become a booming business.

JAPANESE TOURISTS AND *ANNE OF GREEN GABLES*

Perhaps the most unexpected tourists to the Island are the Japanese, who flock to Cavendish to visit Green Gables Heritage Place. In 1996, more than twenty-five thousand Japanese tourists visited the Island, although the decline of the Japanese economy limited this number to three thousand in 2006.

The Japanese were first introduced to Anne by Hanako Muraoka, who wrote the first Japanese translation of *Anne of Green Gables* in 1952. At this time, Japan lay in ruins. The ruling American authorities encouraged Japanese publishers to introduce Western books containing positive, imaginative, and peaceful themes for young readers. Teachers and parents welcomed the fictional Anne as a person who provided readers with a positive role model of how to live in less than ideal circumstances, and *Anne of Green Gables* became part of the elementary school curriculum. Ever since, Anne Shirley has been a part of Japanese culture and Anne books have sold more than thirteen million copies in Japan.

The continued popularity of *Anne of Green Gables* in Japan may be due to the many similarities between Japanese culture and the values and traditions of L. M. Montgomery's fictional setting of Avonlea. The Japanese attraction for *Anne of Green Gables* could also be attributable to the universal appeal of Montgomery's novels. The characters in *Anne of Green Gables*, such as Marilla, with her stern conscience and warm heart; Matthew, who has trouble expressing his feelings; and Anne, whose feelings of rejection and longing for approval are easily identifiable, are recognizable in all places and times.

Getting the Tourists' Dollars

Tourism is the second-largest industry on the Island, boosting the Island economy by hundreds of millions of dollars every year. The number of tourists coming to the Island has gradually increased over the past century, from 11,000 in 1924 to 278,000 in 1963 to 1.4 million in 2007. The latter figure is more than ten times the Island's total population.

Tourists visit the Island to see its signature red soil, green fields, and blue waters, which offer a panorama of beautiful scenic contrasts; bask on one of the Island's many sandy beaches; play a few rounds at one of the Island's many challenging golf courses; or, of course, visit

TREATING TOURISTS RIGHT

In 1973, the Island government placed advertisements in the local newspapers in order to improve Islanders' "tourist manners" and make the Island more tourist-friendly. One ad provided the following tips on hospitality:

- *Speak slowly and distinctly (but don't "shout") when assisting a foreign visitor.*
- *Walk with him a block or more to point out the way.*
- *If he is a photo fan, offer to take a snapshot of him with his camera. Many tourists appreciate this courtesy.*
- *Be enthusiastic and well informed about your local sightseeing attractions.*

the many sites associated with *Anne of Green Gables*. The national park on the Island's north shore is another tourist draw, second in popularity only to Banff National Park in Alberta. The scenic coastline, with its spectacular sand dunes, sandstone cliffs, freshwater ponds, salt marshes, and woodlands, is another major tourist attraction.

Despite the fact that tourism provides many jobs and has become the province's second leading industry, not everyone has been happy with the growing number of tourists visiting the Island. Since the 1908 debate about allowing automobiles on the roads, Islanders have agonized over how much to cater to visitors at the expense of traditional customs. As more and more tourists travel to the Island, traffic jams, parking problems, air pollution, and petty crime threaten to destroy this idyllic environment. At some times, Islanders fight back against the increasing tourist culture on the Island. At other times, however, the jobs created by golf courses, theme parks, and water slides carry the day, and tourist-oriented developments go ahead despite the social and environmental problems they may cause.

The Missing Link

Quicker, safer, and more regular contact with the mainland continued to be an important political issue in the twentieth century. The idea of building a tunnel from the Island to the mainland under the Northumberland Strait was popular from 1884 to 1914, but the project was ultimately too costly and complex in design. The demand for a tunnel died down after the *Prince Edward Island*, a ferry capable of carrying railway cars and automobiles, replaced the *Minto* in 1918. In

1941, Northumberland Ferries Inc. began ferry services between Wood Islands and Caribou, Nova Scotia, giving Islanders another route to the mainland. In later years, the ferry boats that serviced the Island were improved and enlarged—*Abegweit II*, for example, which was in service from 1982 to 1997 between Borden and Cape Tormentine, held 974 passengers, 20 railway cars, and 250 automobiles. Despite these improvements, ferry service to the Island remained slow.

The idea of constructing a bridge or causeway to the mainland reappeared in 1965, when the federal government agreed to build a combined $148-million causeway, bridge, and tunnel. Although work had begun, the federal and provincial governments abandoned the idea in 1969 in favour of a development plan that would distribute the benefits of economic growth more evenly throughout the country.

Interest in a fixed link between the Island and the mainland emerged again in the 1980s. When Island Premier Joe Ghiz called for a plebiscite on this issue in January 1988, Islanders were forced to think about their future. Since a fixed link would affect agriculture (cheaper transportation), fishing (possible environmental damage), tourism (easier access), and the number of visitors to the Island (quality of life), it aroused intense controversy. Although much of the debate focused on economic matters, a major difference was each side's view of "progress." Proponents of the bridge plan, who generally desired the more materialistic lifestyle it would result in, conflicted with those who opposed the bridge in defence of the environment and the "Island way of life."

Almost sixty percent of Islanders voted in favour of some type of a fixed link in the 1988 plebiscite, and in 1993 the federal government engaged Strait Crossing Development Inc. to build a bridge in return for a user toll and an annual subsidy of $42 million, with the stipulation that after thirty-five years of operation, the ownership of the bridge would revert to the federal government.

The engineers from Strait Crossing paid particular attention to the environment during the bridge's construction. To keep the dredging of Northumberland Strait to a minimum, the company used radio signals from several global positioning satellites to place the pier shafts with

Confederation Bridge, the longest bridge over ice-covered water in the world. The project put more than a billion dollars into the economy of Atlantic Canada. The government set aside additional money to compensate the ferry workers and others who would be adversely affected by the bridge, including the towns at either end of the old ferry route, Borden and Cape Tormentine.

an accuracy of two centimetres. The company also developed a 2.2-hectare waterfowl habitat on the mainland and built six osprey nesting platforms on high poles, which quickly doubled the number of nesting pairs of osprey in the area.

The construction of the bridge employed over twenty-four hundred workers at its peak. The maximum elevation above sea level of this cantilevered bridge is sixty metres. To keep drivers alert, the engineers designed three curves in the road help eliminate the hypnotic effect of straight lines. Other safeguards include seventeen emergency call boxes and video surveillance cameras, changeable speed limit and message signs, equipment to monitor wind velocity, and in-pavement sensors to detect ice formation. At a normal driving speed of eighty kilometres per hour, it takes twelve minutes to cross the 12.9 kilometre bridge.

The structure, named Confederation Bridge, opened in June 1997, linking Borden-Carleton with Cape Jourimain, New Brunswick. The construction workers honoured the completion with a sign that read "Dreams Can Come True." Prior to the first day of vehicle traffic, thousands of people lined up for a history-making walk across the bridge.

Although the bridge's social, psychological, and economic impact on the Island is yet to be determined, its immediate impact was a growth in tourism. In 1997, the number of tourists visiting the Island, many of whom were from the Maritimes, surpassed one million for the first time.

The Main Building at the University of Prince Edward Island. The student population at the University of Prince Edward Island has continued to increase, especially with the addition of the Atlantic Veterinary College in 1986. In the 2007–2008 school year, there were approximately four thousand full-time and part-time students enrolled in the university.

Changes in Education

The quality of education on the Island has been a recurrent issue throughout the twentieth century. In 1962, the average teacher's salary in the province was $2,700, compared with the national average of $4,500. Per-capita expenditures for education were the lowest in Canada and fewer than one of every ten teachers had completed university. Another problem was the lack of high schools. Until the 1930s, students had to travel to Charlottetown to take grades 11 and 12.

The response to these problems was school consolidation and school busing in rural areas. Many of the Island's small schools, which had few facilities and had been built decades earlier, were closed and replaced with larger buildings in the 1960s, and the number of one-room schools fell from 470 in 1960 to 57 in 1972. The replacement schools had libraries, gymnasiums, and modern facilities. In step with the rest of Canada, teachers' salaries and the level of teachers' education improved in the last quarter of the century.

Higher education also changed dramatically at the end of the century. During the 1960s, the provincial government wrestled with the contentious subject of university amalgamation. The Island's two institutions of higher learning at that time, the Prince of Wales College and St. Dunstan's College, had developed along different educational philosophies—Prince of Wales College dedicated its efforts to producing students trained in the classics and emphasized high academic standards, while St. Dunstan's College combined Christian ideals with social action and extended its activities into the community. The major debate over the amalgamation was between the supporters of a single public institution, who believed it would help end denominational strife and religious intolerance on the Island, and the proponents of the status quo, who preferred to maintain the two distinctive educational philosophies that were part of the Island's cultural heritage. In 1969, the government united the two colleges into the non-denominational University of Prince Edward Island, which moved into the buildings that had previously been occupied by St. Dunstan's.

Until the late 1960s, the only educational option on the Island for high school graduates was university. As a result, the government established Holland College in 1969 as a community college to satisfy the economic needs of the Island's economy. Built on the Prince of Wales College campus in downtown Charlottetown, Holland College soon created a distinctive role for itself by offering training in practical, job-oriented subjects. In 2007, it had 2,400 full-time and 4,150 part-time students in thirteen locations around the province. Holland College currently operates the provincial vocational high school program, the Atlantic Police Academy, the Culinary Institute of Canada, a paramedics training course, vocational training, a language school, adult night classes, and several other practical programs.

Mi'kmaq girls in sewing class at the Shubenacadie Indian Residential School, 1929. The school provided instruction in farm labour and carpentry for boys and domestic science for girls.

Acadians

The fight for Acadian rights to French-language education continued well into the twentieth century. Despite the best efforts of their leaders, more and more Acadian children attended English-language classes. By 1961, the process of assimilation had progressed so far that less than half of the province's Acadians listed French as their mother tongue, down from seventy-two percent in 1941. By 1966, only one-half of Island Acadians could read or understand French.

In 1980, the tide finally began to turn, as the Island government amended the School Act to allow French education where student numbers warranted. The first area to receive a French-language school was Evangeline. There are now six French-language schools on the Island. Today, many organizations work to ensure the preservation of Acadian heritage and French language, including the Société Saint-Thomas-d'Aquin, La Fédération culturelle de l'Île-du-Prince-Édouard, and The Acadian Museum and Centre for Acadian Research.

Mi'kmaq Education and Culture

Throughout the twentieth century, Aboriginal Peoples in Canada struggled to preserve their cultures in the face of official government policies to assimilate them. In general, Canadian politicians showed little regard for the customs and heritage of the Aboriginal Peoples during most of the twentieth century. For example, Duncan Campbell Scott, head of Indian Affairs in Canada from 1913 to 1932, wrote, "I want to get rid of the Indian problem. Our object is to continue until there is not a single Indian in Canada that has not been absorbed. They are a weird and waning race."

Prior to the late 1940s, unless they were veterans of the Armed Forces (and thus not considered "Indians"), Aboriginal Peoples were denied the right to vote, were prohibited from drinking alcohol, and (until 1957) were not legally considered citizens. Prior to 1985, Aboriginal women who married non-Aboriginals lost their "Indian Status" (as did their offspring), whereas non-Aboriginal women who married "Status Indians" gained Indian Status (as did their children).

Although Lennox Island had its own elementary school, the older Mi'kmaq students who lived there either did not attend high school or had to leave the community for further education. Those who left either attended so-called "white" high schools on Prince Edward Island or the Shubenacadie Indian Residential School in Nova Scotia. Similar to the other 131 Canadian residential schools, the Shubenacadie school, which operated from 1930 to 1967, was designed to assimilate the Aboriginal Peoples—the children were separated from their parents for the school

---

TOO LITTLE, TOO LATE?

In June 2008, Prime Minister Stephen Harper apologized to the former students of the Indian residential school program and decreed that all surviving students of the program were to receive eight thousand dollars in compensation for each year they had lived in a residential school. "The treatment of children in Indian residential schools is a sad chapter in our history..." Harper declared. "Today, we recognize that this policy of assimilation was wrong, has caused great harm, and has no place in our country." Although some Island Mi'kmaq described this historic apology as too little, too late, Darlene Bernard, chief of the Lennox Island Band, responded more positively, declaring, "There was acknowledgment of the damage that was done to our culture and language. To me, that's the very fabric of who we are as a people."

Chuck Strahl, Minister of Indian Affairs and Northern Development and Federal Interlocutor for Métis and Non-Status Indians; Robert Ghiz, Premier of Prince Edward Island; Darlene Bernard, Chief of the Lennox First Nation; and Brian Francis, Chief of the Abegweit First Nation, at a December 2007 meeting in Charlottetown to sign a Canada/Prince Edward Island/Mi'kmaq partnership agreement.

year, instruction was in English, and they were severely punished for speaking their own language and for practising Mi'kmaq cultural and spiritual traditions.

Economic and Political Changes in Mi'kmaq Society

In 1973, the federal government built a causeway to Lennox Island. No longer isolated, and given more freedom by the federal government to administer its own affairs, the Lennox Island First Nation founded an oyster co-op in 1973 and peat moss, handicrafts, and blueberry industries in the 1980s. Another result of the newly granted administrative freedom was the merger of the Morell, Scotchfort, and Rocky Point reserves, which joined together to form the Abegweit First Nation band in 1972 and embarked on their own economic projects.

Today, the Lennox Island First Nation and the Abegweit First Nation bands are governed by elected chiefs and councillors. The Mi'kmaq Confederacy of Prince Edward Island, which was established in 2002 to provide a unified voice for issues concerning both bands, is governed by the chiefs and councils of both communities. The Native Council of Prince Edward Island speaks for non-status and status Aboriginals living off reserve. Each of the three Island counties elects twenty delegates to its annual general assembly, and two representatives to the board of directors. The Island Mi'kmaq continue to work together in the twenty-first century to ensure the protection of their rights and heritage.

NOTABLE TWENTIETH-CENTURY ISLAND POLITICIANS

John Walter Jones (1878-1954) was a prominent Island farmer who was known for starting the seed potato industry on the Island and being a pioneer in adopting modern farming methods. In 1943, Jones was elected premier of Prince Edward Island, and he remained in that position until he was appointed to the federal senate in 1953. During his time as Island premier, "Farmer Jones," as he was often called, championed rural interests, including banning margarine in the province to protect the local dairy industry; replaced Prohibition with government regulation of the sale of intoxicants through the Prince Edward Island Liquor Control Commission; and outlawed unions affiliated with national or international labour organizations. Jones is also remembered for expanding agricultural and fishing services, establishing a forestry program, opening a home for senior citizens, initiating rural electrification, and strengthening education, health care, and social services during his time as premier.

Walter R. Shaw (1887-1981), another farmer premier, sought to return the Island to its farming roots. During his time in power from 1959 to 1966, Shaw established the Prince Edward Island Federation of Agriculture, created a regional high-school system, fostered the development of the food-processing industry, and established a system of bovine tuberculosis testing. He also improved salary and employment conditions in the provincial civil service.

Alexander B. Campbell (1933-) was the longest-serving Island premier. Campbell's time in office, from 1966 to 1978, was a period of enormous economic change. In 1968, the federal government initiated a fifteen-year comprehensive development plan as part of a national policy of distributing the benefits of economic growth more evenly throughout the country. Under Campbell's supervision, the plan changed almost all aspects of the Island's economy, educational system, and government services. In the process, the Island's civil service was professionalized, rural schools were consolidated, restrictions were placed on absentee ownership of land, and renewable energy was given a boost. According to political scientist Wayne Mackinnon, Campbell "laid the foundations for the modernization of Prince Edward Island."

When Islanders elected Joseph Ghiz (1945–1996) as premier in 1986, he became the first Canadian premier of non-European ancestry. During his time as premier, Ghiz was a strong supporter of the Meech Lake and Charlottetown accords, which would have granted the Quebec government special powers in an attempt to suppress the separatist movement. Ghiz's son, Robert, became premier in 2007.

Central Bedeque's Catherine Callbeck (1939–) has lived a pioneering life: she was the only woman in her commerce class at Mount Allison University, the only female business teacher in her school, and the only woman in Alexander B. Campbell's cabinet, where she held two portfolios: Minister of Health and Social Services and Minister Responsible for Disabled Persons. In 1988, Callbeck was elected Member of Parliament for Malpeque, and five years later, she became the first woman to be elected premier of Prince Edward Island. Callbeck retired from her position as premier in 1996, and was appointed to the Senate the following year.

POLITICAL FIRSTS FOR ISLAND WOMEN

1888:   Unmarried women in Charlottetown win the right to vote in municipal elections
1892:   Unmarried women in Summerside win the right to vote in municipal elections
1899:   Women win the right to sit on school boards in Charlottetown and Summerside
1922:   Women win the right to vote in Island elections
1951:   Hilda Ramsay from Indian River is the first female candidate to run for the provincial legislature

1955: Florence Elsie Inman is the first Island woman appointed to the Senate
1960: Mary Bernard is the first woman elected chief of the Lennox Island First Nation
1961: Margaret Mary MacDonald is the first Island woman elected to the House of Commons
1968: Dorothy Corrigan is the first woman elected mayor of Charlottetown
1970: Jean Canfield is the first woman elected to the Island's assembly
1972: Jean Canfield is the first woman Island appointed cabinet minister
1972: Margaret Bernard is elected as the first chief of the newly formed Abegweit Band
1979: Frances Perry is the first woman elected mayor of Summerside
1983: Marion Reid is the first woman to be appointed speaker of the assembly
1986: Eileen Rossiter is the first Island woman appointed to the Senate
1990: Pat Mella becomes the first female leader of a provincial political party (the Progressive Conservative Party)
1990: Marion Reid is the first woman appointed lieutenant-governor of Prince Edward Island
1993: Catherine Callbeck is the first woman elected premier
2004: Lennox Island First Nation elects an all-female band council, including Darlene Bernard as chief
2004: Mildred Dover becomes the first female attorney general in Prince Edward Island

Chapter Fifteen
Contemporary Island Life

Island culture changed radically after the Second World War. Modernization, tensions over land use, a decline in single-family farms, economic difficulties in the fishing industry, dramatic rises in tourism, the construction of Confederation Bridge, and improvement in the education system have all played a role in these cultural changes. "Come from aways" (CFAs) also contributed to the changes in Island life. Beginning in the 1970s and continuing to 2008, more people moved to Prince Edward Island than left, and the percentage of people living on the Island who were born there has decreased. In general, the CFAs were young and well-educated, and they brought new ideas and tastes with them.

Music
Islanders enjoy a wide range of modern musical styles, as well as traditional Scottish, Acadian, and Irish music. Highland step-dancing and fiddling are popular at community *ceilidhs* (a Gaelic word pronounced *KAY-lees*). Islanders have their own distinctive fiddling style, which is a blend of Scottish, Irish, and Acadian elements.

Well-known Island musicians include Angèle Arsenault, Stompin' Tom Connors, Nancy White, Lennie Gallant, and fiddlers Roy Johnstone, Richard Wood, and Cynthia MacLeod. Many Island bands and musicians have national audiences, including Haywire, Two Hours Traffic, Chucky Danger (a.k.a. Paper Lions), Catherine MacLellan, and Gordon Belsher.

Literature
L. M. Montgomery is, of course, is the most widely known Island-born author, but other Island authors have also made their marks in Canada's literary community. Milton Acorn, for example, is one of Canada's mostly highly regarded poets. Dubbed "The People's Poet"

ANNE OF GREEN GABLES ON STAGE

In 1956, the Charlottetown Festival commissioned Don Harron and Norman Campbell to expand their 1956 television version of *Anne of Green Gables* into a full-length musical theatre production. *Anne of Green Gables—The Musical* premiered in 1965 at the Confederation Centre of the Arts in Charlottetown. This musical has been performed at Confederation Centre every summer since 1965, and has played to more than 3.3 million people.

ANNE OF GREEN GABLES: A COMMUNIST PLOT?

At the height of the Cold War, Don Harron was in New York writing lyrics for the CBC television program on *Anne of Green Gables*. After completing his work, Harron used the CBC studios in the United Nations building to send his lyrics to Toronto. However, at this time, Senator Joseph McCarthy was investigating the UN for suspected communist activities, and when his staff saw the words "red" soil and "red" hair, they thought the lyrics were part of a communist code and blocked Harron's transmission.

by fellow poets, he won the Governor General's Literary Award in 1976 for his poetry collection *The Island Means Minago*. Other notable Island poets include John Smith, the Island's first poet laureate and a popular public reader and lecturer; Frank Ledwell, the second poet laureate, who was also a teacher and storyteller; David Helwig, the 2008 poet laureate and a respected fiction writer; and Elaine Harrison, a poet whose work has been adapted and performed in Canada and abroad.

The Island's literary community has always been prominent, and over the years the province has produced a bevy of accomplished writers, including Joseph Sherman, poet and editor of *Arts Atlantic* magazine; Richard Lemm, poet and fiction writer; J. J. Steinfeld, fiction writer and playwright; Kent Stetson, playwright; David Weale, storyteller and nonfiction writer; Hugh MacDonald, poet and prose writer; and Deirdre Kessler, author and poet.

Fine Arts

The Island is home to a vibrant community of artists. Galleries and studios dot the Island countryside. Some of the artists and craftspeople of national and international reputation who currently contribute to the cultural life on the Island include painter Brian Burke, painter and printmaker Henry Purdy, potters Peter Jansons, Malcolm

Stanley, and Hedwig Kolesar, and woodworkers Jacques Gaudreau and Diane Gaudreau.

Hilda Woolnough and Erica Rutherford, two of the Island's most celebrated artists, had an extraordinary influence on the visual arts of Prince Edward Island. Born in Edinburgh, Scotland, Erica Rutherford settled permanently on the Island in 1977. Rutherford worked in theatre and film and was also a printmaker and painter. Rutherford's works are displayed in collections worldwide, and examples of her illustration work can be seen in her books, *The Owl and the Pussycat* and *Yoga for Cats*. Rutherford's autobiography, *Nine Lives*, chronicles her artistic career as well as her personal journey from male to female.

Hilda Woolnough moved to Prince Edward Island in the late 1960s with her husband, Réshard Gool, University of Prince Edward Island political studies professor, writer, poet, and publisher. Woolnough and Gool brought one hundred Canadian writers to the Island, including Margaret Atwood, Pat Lowther, Timothy Findley, and a virtual who's who of the Canadian literature scene to promote the arts. In the late 1990s and early 2000s, Woolnough helped thousands of school children experience the awe and pleasure of making art and observing it at exhibitions in Charlottetown's Arts Guild. Hilda Woolnough's work as printmaker,

WANDA WYATT

Wanda Wyatt, circa 1945

No one was a bigger benefactor to Island arts and culture than Wanda Lefurgey Wyatt. Wanda was a shrewd investor and turned a modest family inheritance into many millions. She donated generously to the Prince Edward Island Museum and Heritage Foundation, the Lefurgey Cultural Centre, Summerside's Wyatt Centre, the College of Piping and Celtic Performing Arts, and the University of Prince Edward Island.

illustrator, painter, and collage artist is known internationally.

Island Athletes

Prince Edward Island has a rich athletic heritage. Islanders do well in such diverse sports as swimming, bobsledding, squash, racquetball, baseball, golf, and hockey. In 1951, Evelyn Henry of Keppoch became the first person to swim the treacherous Northumberland Strait, and in 1999, Barb McNeill conquered the English Channel. In 1998, two-man bobsledder David (Eli) MacEachern brought home the first Olympic gold medal for Prince Edward Island.

Brad Richards accepting the Saskatchewan Junior Hockey League's rookie of the year award, 1997

Jonathon Power, considered one of the greatest shotmakers in the history of squash, started playing the game in Summerside, where his father was director of athletics at the Armed Forces base. He subsequently represented the province at several national junior tournaments before leaving the province and turning professional. In 1999, Power became the first North American squash player to reach the world number one ranking. Over the course of his career, Power has won thirty-six Professional Squash Association titles.

Islanders also keep close tabs on the National Hockey League. As of 2008, twenty-five Islanders have played in the NHL, including Rick Vaive, Gerard Gallant, Forbes Kennedy, Allan MacAdam, Bobby and Billy MacMillan, Errol Thompson, Steve Ott, and Brad Richards. Richards, a native of Murray Harbour, is one of the most successful hockey players to have come from the Island. He was drafted by the Tampa Bay Lightning in 1998, and two years later he made the team and set rookie records for goals (21) and assists (41). In 2004, the Lightning won the Stanley Cup and Richards was awarded the Conn Smythe Trophy as Playoff MVP. That season he

Lori Kane at an Island golf event in 2000

also won the Lady Byng Trophy for sportsmanship and gentlemanly conduct combined with a high standard of playing ability. Later in 2004, Richards led all players in points while playing on Team Canada, which won the World Cup of Hockey. In 2006, Richards played for Team Canada in the Winter Olympics. Two years later, he was traded to the Dallas Stars.

Charlottetown's Lori Kane is another Island athlete who has excelled on the international stage. After an outstanding amateur golfing career, Kane turned professional in 1993 and joined the Ladies Professional Golf Association (LPGA) three years later. Kane is a four-time LPGA winner, and has been selected as Canada's Female Athlete of the Year twice. In 2002, when she received an honorary doctor of laws degree from the University of Prince Edward Island, the university's chancellor commented that Kane's "positive attitude and million-dollar smile have made her one of the best-liked athletes on the tour, a favourite of fans everywhere, and an unofficial ambassador both for Prince Edward Island and for Canada." In 2006, she was presented with the Order of Canada for her charity work with the Boys and Girls Clubs of Canada, Ronald McDonald House Charities, and the KidSport program.

Charlottetown's Charlie Ryan also made his mark in the sports world. Ryan was an all-star catcher and pitcher, umpire, regional scout for the Toronto Blue Jays, coach, and administrator during his long career in baseball. After an impressive playing career at the local, provincial, and regional levels, Ryan coached baseball teams at all levels and helped organize the Charlottetown Baseball league—known from 1986 as the Charlie Ryan Memorial Baseball League. He was Charlottetown's director of recreation from 1966 until his retirement twenty years later. The inscription on his Hillsborough Rotary Club award states: "Charles Ernest Ryan is a man who over the years has given generously of his time and talent in the cause of youth...a man of wit and wisdom, a sportsman, a family man, a community man, a veteran, a Legionnaire, and a true leader who in his interaction with youth has provided a fine example for all to follow."

Charlie Ryan

Harness Racing

Harness racing is rooted deep in Prince Edward Island's history and is an integral part of its agricultural heritage. Beginning with the pioneer settlers, farmers raced their best horses against one another for pride and money. By the 1880s, the Island had more than two dozen racing tracks, including Summerside Raceway, which is reputed to be the oldest-existing track in Canada.

JOE O'BRIEN: HARNESS RACER

Alberton's Joe O'Brien was one of North America's premier harness racers. He drove more sub-two-minute miles than any other harness driver in history. O'Brien won his first race at the Summerside track in 1933, at age sixteen. After fourteen years of driving success, O'Brien moved to the United States, where he won 4,285 races, captured the Kentucky Futurity five times, and won the Hambletonian and the Little Brown Jug races twice each. In 1940, O'Brien proved his ability as a trainer by taking Dudey Patch, a broken-down eleven-year-old horse, and turning him into a Canadian champion.

Dr. J. D. MacIntyre rides Lady Belle on the Montague racetrack, 1919

The introduction of night pari-mutuel racing at the Charlottetown Driving Park in 1946 brought an end to many of the smaller Island tracks, and more recently, the lure of video lottery terminals as a convenient form of gambling has further reduced attendance. Each August since 1961, the crowning harness racing event of the year has been the Gold Cup and Saucer Race at the Old Home Week agricultural fair in Charlottetown.

The People

With a population of approximately 140,000 people inhabiting 1,404,547 acres, Prince Edward Island has the highest provincial population density in Canada. More than forty percent of the province is farmland, and one feels the closeness of countryside and ocean from almost everywhere on the Island. In 2008, the province's only two cities, Charlottetown and Summerside, contained 32,250 and 14,650 people, respectively. With a population of just over 7,000, Stratford is the largest town. The rural backbone of Prince Edward Island consists of seven towns and sixty-six outlying municipalities, of which about twenty are considered historic villages.

Although people with a wide variety of ethnic origins have immigrated to the Island since the Second World War, Prince Edward

Island remains the most homogeneous population in Canada. Despite the overwhelming British and French ethnic composition of the population, Prince Edward Island has a strong multicultural community that includes people from approximately eighty nationalities.

Political Culture on the Island

Prince Edward Island politics reflect the narrow confines of the Island—the provincial legislature is smaller than either the Montreal or Toronto city councils. Local political meetings are generally well-attended, giving Islanders a sense that their opinions and actions can directly affect the way the province is governed—which helps explain why Prince Edward Island usually has the highest voting turnout ratio in Canada. For example, although the 2003 election was the day after Hurricane Juan knocked out power to much of the Island, voter turnout still exceeded eighty percent.

Since joining Confederation, Prince Edward Island has had a two-party government. When New Democratic Party member Herb Dickieson was elected in 1996, he became the first and only successful third-party candidate in the province. Except for the period between 1891 and 1911, and again between 1935 and 1959, the Liberal and Conservative parties regularly switched between government and opposition. Since 1935, no Island government has failed to win a second term in office.

Island politics are often characterized by extreme partisanship. Most people feel a personal connection to either the Liberal or Conservative party, and expect their children to inherit their political beliefs. Almost everyone knows their elected representatives either personally or through a friend or colleague. Since ridings tend to be quite small, electioneering is fought house-to-house rather than on television. Until recently, when rulings based on the Charter of Rights and Freedoms restricted blatant political favouritism, political issues were often dominated by discussions over patronage. Although the problem of absentee landlords was resolved more than a century ago, Island politics still revolve around such land-related issues as crop rotation, soil runoff, high levels of pesticide and fertilizer, and non-resident landowners.

While the Island might seem over-governed for a province of only 138,600 people, it possesses a sort of direct democracy. Each elected member to the provincial government, for example, represents about 5,000 citizens. In Ontario, by contrast, each provincial member serves over 70,000 people.

As Prince Edward Island approaches the second decade of the twentieth century, it faces many challenges. Will the Island be able to control its own destiny with increasing globalism? Already, the information highway is blurring the distinction between urban and rural and Island and off-Island. Agriculture and tourism seem destined to lead the economy for the foreseeable future, but what impact will they have on the environment? Still, perhaps maintaining the Island way of life, "The Gentle Island" as the tourism slogan states, is worth the effort.

Appendix

A History of Prince Edward Island in Postage Stamps

The following Canadian postage stamps illustrate some of the major themes in Prince Edward Island history.

© copyright Canada Post {1989}

Canada Post used the anonymous painting (circa 1820–1830) depicted in this 1989 stamp to portray the Algonquian-speaking people (Ojibwa, Cree, Algonquin, Montagnais, Mi'kmaq and Maliseet) who occupied the Maritimes, Quebec, northern Ontario, and parts of the Prairies before European exploration.

© copyright Canada Post {2006}

Champlain sailed a small, two-masted barque such as the one depicted in this stamp to chart the east coast of North America in 1606. Given the journey's historical importance to both countries, this 2006 stamp commemorating the four hundredth anniversary of Champlain's voyage was a joint issue with the United States.

© copyright Canada Post {2005}

This 2005 stamp marked the 250th anniversary of the Acadian Deportation. The Grand Pré stamp in the centre was issued to mark the Deportation's 175th anniversary in 1930.

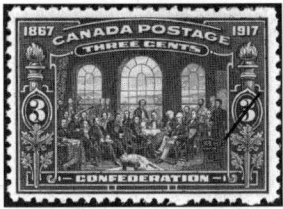

© copyright Canada Post {1917}

This 1917 stamp, which was based on Robert Harris's original oil painting of the Fathers of Confederation, commemorates the fiftieth anniversary of Confederation. Eight Fathers of Confederation in the original painting were left out on the stamp for space and balance concerns. This omission was later rectified in a 1927 stamp.

© copyright Canada Post {1987}

In 1852, British engineer Frederick Newton Gisborne laid North America's first undersea cable between New Brunswick and Prince Edward Island. This stamp, issued for Canada Day 1987, was part of a science and technology series celebrating Canadian innovations in communications.

© copyright Canada Post {1978}

This 1978 stamp depicts *Northern Light*, the first Canadian government steamer, which entered service in 1876. *Northern Light*, which was one of the Island's rewards for entering Confederation, ferried passengers and mail between Prince Edward Island and Nova Scotia from 1876 to 1888.

© copyright Canada Post {1943}

This 1943 stamp commemorates the signing of the British Commonwealth Air Training Plan in 1939. Under this plan, administered by the Royal Canadian Air Force, men from all parts of the British Commonwealth and its allies were trained in schools established across the country. Island bases trained more than twelve thousand pilots during the Second World War.

© copyright Canada Post {1979}

In 1979, Canada Post issued this stamp as part of a twelve-stamp series as a reminder that a country with the strength of unity behind it, and with an outstanding record, can face the future with confidence. According to tradition, the large oak depicted on the stamp, part of the arms of Prince Edward Island, represents England, and the saplings represent the three counties of the Island.

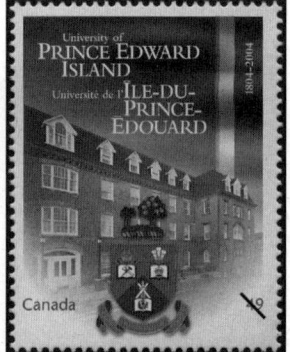

© copyright Canada Post {1980}

This 1980 stamp commemorates the two hundredth anniversary of the University of Prince Edward Island.

© copyright Canada Post {1993}

This stamp was issued as part of a twelve-stamp series depicting provincial and territorial parks, which was released to celebrate Canada Day in 1993. Cedar Dunes Park contains some of the most beautiful beaches on the Island, which attract droves of tourists every year.

This 1997 stamp commemorates the official opening of Confederation Bridge on May 31, 1997.

© *copyright Canada Post {1997}*

This 2005 stamp depicting a winter scene near New Glasgow is part of a series of stamps representing Canada's geographic diversity.

© *copyright Canada Post {2005}*

Image Sources

Ken Shelton/Tea Hill Press: 1, 25, 40, 41, 53

Rhoda Knight Kalt: 2

Library and Archives Canada: 7, 11, 18, 47, 58, 76, 77, 92, 96 (t & b), 97, 99, 107(b), 147, 149(t), 154, 155, 168, 180, 199

Nimbus Publishing: 12, 128 (l & r), 139, 192

Nova Scotia Archives and Records Management: 16, 17

Earle Lockerby: 29

Dalhousie University Library: 31

Private Collection of Rollo: 33

Bibliothèque Nationale de France: 35

Public Archives and Records Office of Prince Edward Island (PARO): Page 38—Acc.2320/6-4 (page 4); Page 54—Acc.3466/72.66.1.7; Page 59—Acc.2320/25-2; Page 66—Acc.2330/H-87; Page 75—Map 0534; Page 80—Acc.2230/54-7; Page 81—Acc.2702/6; Page 88—Acc.2301/301; Page 89—Acc.2320/60-8; Page 91—Acc.2755/120; Page 105—Acc.3466/HF 70.499 p. 6, middle of booklet; Page 113—Acc4339/1; Page 114—Acc.3466/HF74.285.26; Page 117—Acc.2301/15; Page 121—Acc.3148/10; Page 126—Acc.3218/80; Page 132—Acc.3466/HF72.66.4.45; Page 142—Acc.2320/32-14; Page 149(b)—Acc.2320/103-3; Page 160—Acc.4391/1; Page 176—Acc.4296/Series 9/1; Page 182—Acc.4086/1; Page 211—Acc.2476/6/40-2

Provincial Archives of Manitoba: 46

Confederation Centre Art Gallery and Museum: 60, 63, 69, 70, 83, 107(t), 115

Province of Nova Scotia: 85

Topley Studio, c/o Library and Archives Canada: 106, 111

Doug Murray, Postal Historian: 110, 116, 119, 133, 175

Karen Gallant: 137

Department of Mines and Resources, c/o Library and Archives Canada: 144

Gallant, Gerard, and Florence: 166

Sears Photography: 169

Wyatt Heritage Properties: 184, 207

UPEI Photography: 197

PEI Gov't / Brian L. Simpson: 201, 209

Athol College of Notre Dame Archives: 208

PEI Sports Hall of Fame: 210

Appendix images (pages 214–217) reproduced with permission from Canada Post Corporation. All images © copyright of Canada Post.